THE EXPERTS REV
BEATING TH

HOW TO
WIN AT
Everything

Dan Bensimhon

 Bantam Books   New York Toronto London Sydney Auckland

HOW TO WIN AT EVERYTHING
A Bantam Book / January 1996

Library of Congress Cataloging-in-Publication Data
How to win at everything : experts reveal the fine art of beating the
competition / Dan Bensimhon.
    p.   cm.
    ISBN 0-553-37461-3
    1. Success—Handbooks, manuals, etc.   2. Self-actualization
(Psychology)—Handbooks, manuals, etc.   3. Life skills—
Handbooks, manuals, etc.   I. Bensimhon, Dan.
BJ1611.H68   1995
646.7—dc20   95-15240
                                                          CIP
Published simultaneously in the United States and Canada

PRINTED IN THE UNITED STATES OF AMERICA
FFG   10 9 8 7 6 5 4 3 2 1

CONTENTS

INTRODUCTION   vii

FITNESS AND HEALTH

Getting in Shape Quickly   2
Sticking with an
  Exercise Program   5
Building a Good Physique   7
Losing Weight   9
Quitting Smoking   12
Preventing a Heart Attack   14
Lowering Your Blood Pressure   17

MONEY AND BUSINESS

Beating a Bad Credit Report   20
Getting a Raise   22

Becoming a Good Manager   25
Saving for Retirement   28
Starting Your Own Business   31
  How Ben & Jerry Did It   34
Playing the Stock Market   35
Beating a Tax Audit   39
Buying a New Car   41
Buying a Used Car   45
Paying Less in Taxes   47
Buying a House   51
  How to Make a Structural
  Inspection   55
Selling Your House   57
Getting Good Airline Fares   60

SPORTS

Arm Wrestling   66

Contents

Bass Fishing 68
Bowling 70
Softball 72
Flag Football 75
Running 77
  Marathon Training 79
Cycling 83
  Century Training 86
Fly Fishing 89
Basketball 92
Getting Good Playoff Seats 94
Triathlon 96
Volleyball 99
Tennis 101
Swimming 104
Racquetball 107
Mountain Biking 109
Golf 112

GAMES

Nintendo 116
Eating Contests 118

Shooting Pool 120
Rotisserie League Baseball 122
Beer Chugging 125
Monopoly 127
Lottery 129
Betting on the Horses 130
Poker 132
Football Pools 134
Blackjack 136
Chess 139
Crossword Puzzles 141
Darts 143

LIVING

Getting a Good Shave 146
Giving a Good Speech 148
  The Ten Best Speeches
  Ever Given 151
Talking Your Way Out of
  a Speeding Ticket 152
Holding Your Own in a Fight 154
Training Your Dog 156

Buying a Suit   159
Getting Your Kid into College   161
Brewing Beer   163

RELATIONSHIPS

Making Conversation   166
Picking Up a Woman in a Bar   168
  Best Pick-up Lines for
    Different Situations   171

Making Dinner for a Woman   174
Making Love to a Woman   177
Raising Good Kids   179
Making Up (Without Losing
  Your Pride)   182

Introduction

Face it, life is war. Whether you're up for a promotion, locking horns on the gridiron, or just trying to get a better deal on a new car, it's always you against the next guy. Mano a mano. While some guys can convince themselves that coming in second isn't so bad after all, true champions see it otherwise. Just ask Larry Csonka, the Hall of Fame fullback, who once said, "Just thinking about losing is enough incentive for me to win."

Granted, in most instances *someone* has to lose, but with the right strategy and a few tricks up your sleeve, that someone doesn't have to be *you*. To help you get the winning edge, we've fast-talked and wheedled our way into the confidences of some of the world's most successful athletes, businessmen, and scientists—not to mention the finest beer brewers and most prosperous poker players. We kept asking them for their secrets to success until they knuckled under and told us what they've learned on their climb to the top.

We discovered time and time again that the difference between winning and losing isn't as insurmountable as it may seem. "You only have to do one or two things differently to beat 50 percent of the players who are now beating you," says Vic Braden, teaching pro and founder of the world-famous Vic Braden Tennis College. So, sit back, prop your feet up and learn how to turn the tables on your opponents. Because if winning isn't everything, why bother keeping score?

FITNESS AND HEALTH

Getting in Shape Quickly

Dan Harvey
Robert DeNiro's personal trainer

1. Be consistent. "More than anything, you have to do a little something—even if it's only running a mile—at least four or five times a week," says Harvey. "Going to the gym six days one week and two the next isn't going to get the job done."

2. Relax. In order to see positive results, you need to give your body time to rebuild after each workout. "Recovery time is just as important as workout time," says Harvey. Even on a crash course, you need one or two days off a week, especially after hard workouts.

3. Cross-train. When starting an exercise program, include both strength training and cardiovascular exercise. "One provides the base for the other, so you'll see gains more quickly," says Harvey. If your main focus is to lose weight, 60 to 70 percent of your workout time should be devoted to cardiovascular training, like running, cycling, stair climbing or brisk walking. If you're already thin and want more muscle tone, reverse the percentages.

4. Repeat yourself. When you first start weight lifting, it's better to do many repetitions with light weights than few repetitions with heavy ones. "Not only is there less chance of injury, but the high reps allow you to get by with only a little rest between sets, so you condition your muscles and cardiovascular system at the same time," says Harvey. For the first four weeks do 15 to 20 repetitions per set (with one to two minutes rest between sets). As you progress, you can cut back to 8 to 12 reps to focus more on strength and size.

5. Don't do it all in one day. If you're lifting four days a week, work your chest, shoulders and triceps on one day and your back, biceps and legs the next. Then take a day off and repeat the cycle. Splitting up your weight training this way keeps you more focused and gives you a better workout, says Harvey. If you're working out six days a week, work your legs on a separate day and go three on, one off.

6. Work up to it. To build up your running endurance, start by alternating one minute of easy running with one minute of slow jogging or walking. Then gradually cut the jogging/walking time in half until you can run continuously for 30 to 40 minutes. The same principle works for other aerobic activities like biking, stair climbing and swimming.

7. Have a plan. Once you have enough endurance to handle 40 minutes of cardiovascular exercise comfortably, schedule one or two longer, slower cardiovascular workouts (50 minutes to one hour) each week. That will teach your body to burn fat more efficiently. Another one or two days, do shorter "interval" workouts to crank up your speed and metabolism. A simple interval workout would look like this: After warming up for five minutes at an easy pace, up your intensity for one minute. Go easy for a minute to recover, then pick it up again. Alternate for 20 minutes and finish with a five-minute cooldown. Spend your remaining days doing 30 to 40 minutes of easy-to-moderate activity.

8. Mix it up. Whether you're weight lifting or working on your cardiovascular system, you'll see the most benefit by switching exercises frequently. "Not only will it help keep you motivated, but it will develop your muscles more completely," says Harvey. "If you've been doing bench presses every week, switch to a week or two of push-ups or dumbbell presses, and don't just sit on a bike five days a week—get on the treadmill or stair climber."

9. Focus on your diet. What you eat has as much, if not more, to do with how you look than how much you work out. "No matter how hard you exercise, you're not going to get optimal results if you're eating like a glutton," says Harvey. Shoot for a diet that gives you 2,000 to 2,500 calories a day, is low in fat and has plenty of complex carbohydrates. "Any lower than that, and you won't have the energy you need to sustain high-quality workouts," says Harvey.

10. Watch the pasta. Sure, Mama Leone's specialty is high in carbos, but chances are, even her marinara is loaded with olive oil—which is 100 percent fat. Ask for all your sauces and dressings on the side, or better yet, buy nonfat versions at the store.

Sticking with an Exercise Program

Bob Ray
U.S. record holder for longest running streak. Ray has run at least four miles a day, every day, since April 4, 1967.

1. Work out in the morning. If you exercise before you go to the office, there's less chance you'll miss a workout because of a late meeting or an unscheduled appointment.

2. Find a training partner or join a running club. "It's a lot harder to skip a workout when you have to explain yourself to someone else," says Ray. Besides, having someone to chat with makes the time go quicker.

3. Bet on yourself. Studies have shown that if you make a bet with friends or coworkers, you're more likely to keep up a streak. "Men are naturally competitive," says Ray. "Take advantage of it."

4. Start slow. "Trying to do too much too soon will kill your motivation inside of two weeks and probably leave you injured," says Ray. Start your program by walking for 20 to 30 minutes, three to four times a week. Then try alternating walking and running during your workouts. Do that for 6 months before you become a full-fledged runner. The same gradual buildup works for any aerobic sport, including swimming and cycling. "The steady improvement you'll see is enough to keep you coming back," says Ray.

5. Cross-train. Alternating among a few different sports will keep you from getting bored. Ten minutes on the treadmill, followed by 10 minutes on a stationary bike and another 10 on the stair climber will give you just as good a workout—if not better—as spending 30 minutes on any one of them.

6. Keep an exercise diary. Recording your miles or the time you spend exercising every day will help keep you motivated—and honest, says Ray. "If you see too many zeros in your weekly totals, it's a sure sign you have to do more." And an exercise diary can often help you figure out whether an injury was caused by a change in shoes or other equipment, running too many hills or simply overdoing it.

7. Set short-term goals. Goals you can reach in one week to a month are better for keeping you motivated than more long-term goals. "When I first started my streak, my goal was to run for two weeks straight," says Ray.

8. Just get started. On days when you don't feel up to the task, tell yourself you're going to exercise for only 10 or 15 minutes. "Nine times out of ten, you'll feel better, and go longer, once you get out the door," says Ray. "But if you still feel bad after 10 minutes, call it a day."

Building a Good Physique

Bill Pearl
Former Mr. Universe and author of *Getting Stronger*
(Shelter Publications, 1986)

1. Start big. It's best to begin every workout targeting your largest muscle groups—quads, hamstrings, chest and back. Then progress to the smaller ones—biceps, shoulders, triceps and calves. The reason? When you work your large muscles, your smaller muscles get called in to help support the load. If you've already fatigued them, they're likely to call it quits before you've taxed your main muscle groups sufficiently.

2. Lift late. Your body temperature, blood pressure and testosterone levels peak late in the afternoon, allowing you to work harder and benefit more from after-work workouts.

3. Use the buddy system. A training partner can help get you to the gym and maintain your intensity on days when you'd rather be captaining the couch.

4. Mix it up. "Your muscles adapt to an exercise inside of two months," says Pearl. To avoid plateauing, change your routine regularly by switching exercises, increasing the weight or number of sets, or swapping your barbell for a set of dumbbells or a machine. "Every six to eight weeks, do a complete overhaul," says Pearl.

5. Strength and size aren't the same thing. If you're primarily interested in building the size of your muscles, figure on doing several sets with moderate weight, for example, four or five sets of 8 to 12 repetitions. Whereas, if you're looking for brute strength, increase the weight and cut down the number of sets and reps so that you're somewhere in the neighborhood of doing three sets of 5 to 8 repetitions.

6. Don't megadose on supplements. "Most Americans get more protein than they can use from their diets," says Pearl. "The extra calories are likely to wind up on your waist, not your biceps."

7. Be consistent. "You'll get more results from three or four smaller work–outs per week than one or two marathon sessions," says Pearl. Forty-five minutes three times a week is sufficient for novices, but if you've been at it for more than six months you'll need to up your gym time to keep packing on the muscle.

8. But don't forget to rest. Your muscles can take 48 hours or more to recover after a hard workout. So targeting each body part more than three times a week may actually be counterproductive. If you want to lift five or six days a week, split up your workouts so that you're not blasting the same muscle groups on consecutive days.

Losing Weight

Morton Shaevitz, Ph.D.
Associate clinical professor of psychiatry, University of California—San Diego School of Medicine
Author, *Lean and Mean: The No-Hassle Life-Extending Weight Loss Program for Men* (G.P. Putnam, 1993)

1. Cut the fat. Since fat has more than twice as many calories per gram as either carbohydrates or protein, cutting it out of your diet is the quickest way to lose weight. "By making three simple changes, you can easily cut the fat in your diet in half," says Shaevitz. 1) *Sprinkle* cheese on your food only as a flavoring. Avoid foods smothered in cheese or with it baked through them. 2) Replace red meat entrées with skinless poultry or fish. 3) Order all dressings and sauces on the side and use them for light dipping, not as a swimming pool.

2. Don't deprive yourself. If you absolutely have to have that doughnut with your afternoon coffee, do it. "If you feel like you've really missed out, you're going to stop off and get a double-pepperoni pizza on the way home," says Shaevitz.

3. Learn how to eat in public. "Most men eat two to three of their daily meals away from home," says Shaevitz. That makes it hard to control what you eat. For example, if you're going to a breakfast meeting where doughnuts and muffins are likely to be your only options, eat before you go or take something with you. If you're caught unprepared, skimp on anything that's fried or is drowning in sauce and load up on bread and potatoes (without butter), fruits and vegetables. On airplanes, always order special low-fat or seafood meals ahead of time.

4. You don't have to be a rabbit. A steak dinner once or twice a week is OK, as long as you don't go for Cowboy Bob's superside of beef. "Cut the steak in half and double up on the baked potato—without sour cream," says Shaevitz. "After a while, you'll find that when you cut the fat, you can eat more food and still lose weight."

5. Exercise. Don't even try to lose weight without working out. Slowly build up to the point where you're working out 45 to 60 minutes, five to six times a week. Once you lose the weight, you can cut back to 30 to 45 minutes, four to five times a week. "You won't exercise if you try to *find* the time," says Shaevitz. "You have to *make* time, as you would for a business meeting."

6. Skimp on the iron. While lifting weights will tone you up, weight lifting doesn't torch many calories. "If you have less than an hour a day for exercise, use most of the time for aerobic exercise, like walking, cycling or swimming," says Shaevitz. "If you have a few minutes left over, throw in some circuit-weight training."

7. Don't starve yourself. "Men are volume eaters," says Shaevitz. "It's almost impossible to stick to a diet when you're eating less than 1,500 calories a day."

8. Be realistic. Using these tactics, you can expect to lose about two pounds a week fairly comfortably. Try to lose it more quickly and you're likely to be miserable. Go for much less and you probably won't see enough of a weekly payoff to stick with it.

9. Chart your progress. Make a graph that compares your actual weight loss with your predicted weight loss. "That's a great way for men to lose weight—it makes weight loss a competition," says Shaevitz. Keeping a log of your workouts is also a good stimulus for exercising regularly. "Pretty soon you forget about trying to lose weight and you focus on going faster or longer than last week's workout," he says.

10. Don't drink. For many men, alcohol is a major source of calories. To make matters worse, booze also hinders the body's ability to metabolize fat. "I know it's a radical position, but I tell my patients not to drink any alcohol when they're trying to lose weight," says Shaevitz. If teetotaling isn't for you, limit yourself to one to two drinks a day and avoid hard alcohol and frozen drinks, which are loaded with calories.

11. Stay away from the buffet. Even salad bars are loaded with fat-laden cheeses, mayonnaise, sauces and dressings.

12. Take a breather. "Most men use food to beat stress, boredom and anger," says Shaevitz. So after the boss dumps a big project in your lap or you have a fight with your wife, give yourself a few minutes to relax or take a short walk down the hall. If you're still hungry when you're done, then you can grab a bite.

Quitting Smoking

John Pierce, Ph.D.
Smoking researcher and program director, Cancer Prevention and
Control Program, University of California, San Diego

1. Put off your first cigarette. If you can wait 30 minutes after you wake before lighting up, you have more than three times the chance of quitting than someone who can't. "If you have to put a cigarette in your mouth before you roll over and look at your wife, you'll have a tough time quitting," says Pierce.

2. Practice quitting. "With each attempt you get some practice at coping without cigarettes," says Pierce. "The people who have the best odds of quitting for good are those who have stayed off cigarettes for at least a week in the past year. It's like running a marathon—you can't just go out and run 26 miles without training for it." Try to go without for at least a week. Anything less doesn't do much to improve your confidence or lower your addiction, says Pierce.

3. Cut down gradually. Weaning yourself from smoking a pack a day to under 15 cigarettes a day more than doubles your odds of quitting. "The less nicotine you're getting, the fewer withdrawal symptoms you'll have and the easier it'll be to quit," says Pierce.

4. If you're under 15 cigarettes, go cold turkey. "Once you get down to six or eight cigarettes a day, chances are you'll treat them as precious rewards," says Pierce. "So mentally, it becomes almost impossible to give them up."

5. If you're really addicted, try one strategy at a time. If you smoke more than a pack a day, have to light up as soon as your eyes open *and* have never quit for more than a week, trying to remedy all three at once will cripple your chances of succeeding, says Pierce. And the severity of your withdrawal symptoms will probably keep you from trying again.

6. Get someone to look over your shoulder. As your high-school football coach can tell you, having someone to push you when you're tired can make a seemingly impossible task possible. "It can really help, especially in the first few days after you quit," says Pierce.

7. Don't rely on the patch alone. While a nicotine patch can help you beat your physiological dependency, it does little for your psychological addiction. "You need to figure out a way to deal with the stresses that make you reach for a cigarette in the first place," says Pierce. Taking a walk, calling a friend or just meditating for a second can help you break the tension when you feel the urge to light up.

8. Don't underestimate the task. "The biggest mistake smokers make is underestimating how hard it actually is to quit, and they wind up going about it the wrong way," says Pierce. "It took you years to develop the habit— it's going to take you a while to quit."

Preventing a Heart Attack

Dean Ornish, M.D.
Cardiac researcher, founder of the Preventive Medicine Research Institute in Sausalito, California, and author of *Eat More, Weigh Less* (HarperCollins, 1993) and *Dr. Dean Ornish's Program for Reversing Heart Disease* (Random House, 1990)

1. Manage stress. "Reducing the anxiety and stress in your life is an important factor in avoiding a heart attack," says Dr. Ornish. "Once you control stress, everything else becomes easier—quitting smoking, losing weight, exercising regularly." Put aside at least a few minutes every day for meditation. "Doing so allows you to accomplish more without getting as stressed and sick in the process."

2. Build bridges. "Studies have shown that people who are socially isolated have three to five times the risk of premature death from heart attacks and other serious diseases than those who have a sense of connection and community," says Dr. Ornish. The goal is to have someone with whom you feel safe enough to be yourself and still feel loved and supported. "Ask yourself, 'If my house burns down at 3 A.M., is there someone whom I can stay with for a week or two?' If the answer is no, or you had to think about it, you need to work on building friendships where you can talk openly."

3. Start young. People who start eating a low-fat diet, managing stress and exercising regularly when they're in their 20s and 30s rarely have to be as vigilant with their lifestyle as people who've made the healthy changes later in life. "Heart disease is progressive. The earlier you start preventing it, the easier it is to avoid it," says Dr. Ornish.

4. Quit smoking. Hands down, cigarette smoking is the single biggest risk factor for heart disease. Not to mention what it will do to your lungs.

5. Cut your cholesterol. For every one percent you reduce your total cholesterol level, your risk of dying from a heart attack goes down two percent. And although your body has the ability to make cholesterol on its own, the number-one way to reduce your level is not to eat it or saturated fats—which can be easily converted to cholesterol. The biggest sources of cholesterol—and the easiest places to cut it out of your diet—are red meat, processed lunch meats, egg yolks, mayonnaise and high-fat dairy products (ice cream, whole milk, butter and cheese). In addition, all oils are 100 percent fat and should be avoided—including olive oil, which is 14 percent saturated fat. "Heart attacks are almost nonexistent in people with a total cholesterol level under 150," says Dr. Ornish.

6. Go easy on the exercise. Studies have shown you don't have to be as fit as a marathoner to be heart healthy. In fact, walking for 30 minutes four or five times a week provides just about all the heart-attack-reducing benefits of even the most rigorous exercise programs. "The main benefit to your heart health comes from going from no exercise to regular walking," says Dr. Ornish. "Running might make you fitter, but it won't do much more than walking to lower your heart disease risk."

7. Cut the fat. Most weight-loss diets don't work because they're based on deprivation tactics like counting calories and restricting portion sizes. In fact, within five years, 97 percent of the people who lose weight gain it all back. And this yo-yo pattern of weight gain and weight loss may be harmful to your heart. But you can significantly increase your chances of losing weight and keeping it off—and thus cut your heart disease risk—by changing the *type* of food you eat, not the *amount*. If you're getting only 10 percent of your daily calories from fat, you can eat whenever you're hungry and lose weight that you're not likely to see again, says Dr. Ornish.

8. Take radical measures. Conventional wisdom says that small changes are easy and big changes are hard. But we've found that when people make only slight changes in their diet they still feel deprived and don't manage to put much of a dent in their heart attack risk, says Dr. Ornish. On the other hand, people who started exercising and worked to reduce their stress in addition to almost completely overhauling their diets—to focus on complex carbohydrates, nonfat dairy products, fruits, vegetables, egg whites and legumes—usually feel so much better, so quickly, that the change is much easier.

Lowering Your Blood Pressure

Ray Gifford Jr., M.D.
Chairman of the Fifth Joint National Committee on Detection, Evaluation and Treatment of High Blood Pressure for the National Heart, Lung and Blood Institute

1. Lose weight. For most people, dropping a few pounds through a combination of diet and exercise is the most effective way to reduce high blood pressure. "Even if you're 40 pounds overweight, losing just 10 or 15 of it can be enough to bring your blood pressure into normal range," says Dr. Gifford.

2. Blow off smoking. Although smoking itself won't raise your blood pressure, high blood pressure and smoking work synergistically to raise your risk of cardiovascular disease.

3. Be an aerobic animal. "Aerobic exercise will lower your blood pressure regardless of whether or not you lose weight," says Dr. Gifford. On the other hand, weight lifting can actually raise your blood pressure slightly. So until you get your blood pressure to a normal level, it's best to skip the weights and focus on activities like walking, running, cycling, swimming and stair climbing.

4. Bust your stress before it happens. One study suggests that by exercising before a stressful event you can actually reduce how high your blood pressure rises during the stress period. So if you're scheduled for a 10 A.M. meeting with the boss, getting in an early-morning jog may help you keep your pressure in check. "There's no research I know of that shows it will have any long-term benefits," says Gifford. "But it can't hurt."

5. Don't be a salt. Fifty percent of all hypertensives are sensitive to salt—the more they eat, the higher their blood pressure. And contrary to what you may think, the majority of your salt intake probably doesn't come from the shaker, says Dr. Gifford. Lunch meats, cereals, salad dressings, canned foods and snacks are all sodium mines. Choosing low-sodium alternatives, rinsing canned foods in water and eating fresh meats, fruits and vegetables are your best ways to cut your salt intake.

6. Don't say no to drugs. If your blood pressure won't come down after a few weeks of exercise and dieting, an antihypertensive drug may be in order. "No matter how you do it, lowering your blood pressure will reduce your risk of heart attack and stroke," says Dr. Gifford.

7. Have a drink. "Teetotalers tend to have higher blood pressures than moderate drinkers," says Dr. Gifford. A drink or two a day (no more) may actually be good for your blood pressure.

8. Skip the minerals. Over the past few years, some scientists have theorized that minerals like calcium, potassium and magnesium may actually help reduce blood pressure. But there's little scientific proof, says Dr. Gifford. For the best results, stick to tried-and-true tactics like weight loss, exercise and salt restriction.

MONEY AND BUSINESS

Beating a Bad Credit Report

Greg Daugherty
Economics editor, *Consumer Reports* magazine

1. Don't duck bill collectors. Most companies are more interested in getting their money than reporting you to a credit agency. If you can't pay a bill on time, call the company to see if you can work out a payment program.

2. Use your full name. Credit bureaus sometimes mix up the credit information on people with similar names. To minimize the chance of this happening to you, register all your accounts in your full name—middle name included.

3. Check your credit before you need it. Being turned down for a loan because of a bad credit report—even if there's a mistake—isn't fun. And since it typically takes three weeks or more to fix errors, contact *all* three major credit bureaus for a copy of your report at least a month before you go for a loan. To get a copy of each of your reports, call Equifax Credit Information Services at (800) 685-1111, TRW at (800) 682-7654 and Trans Union National Consumer Relations Disclosure Center at (800) 851-2674.

4. Don't go to a credit doctor. The credit repair clinics advertised on late-night TV are usually a scam. "If there's inaccurate information on your credit report, you can have it removed without their help," says Daugherty. "And there's nothing anyone can legally do for you to have a legitimate credit problem removed early." If you're having problems, contact your lawyer.

5. Recheck your report. Errors have a way of creeping back into credit reports even after they've been "corrected," says Daugherty. After having a mistake fixed, request another report—from all three companies—three months down the road.

6. Know the limit. All delinquent accounts must be removed from your credit report after seven years, except for bankruptcies, which can be on the books for ten years.

7. Ask why you were turned down. "If you're denied credit, you have the right to ask where the lender got the information that gave you the bad rap," says Daugherty. If it's a mistake, get a copy of your report from each bureau. "If there's an error in one, there may be an error in all of them."

8. Save your canceled checks for at least seven years. The only way to successfully dispute a company's contention that your payment was delinquent is to have proof.

Getting a Raise

William Ury, Ph.D.
Associate director, Program on Negotiation, Harvard Law School, and author of *Getting Past No: Negotiating Your Way from Confrontation to Cooperation* (Bantam, 1991)

1. Make your boss's problem your problem. The biggest mistake you can make in a salary negotiation is to treat your boss as an adversary. Instead, help him figure out a way to give you a raise and still meet his budget or be able to explain it to *his* boss.

2. Invent options. If your boss says no because of low cash flow, be ready with other ways in which he can reward you—like letting you have a few extra vacation days, moving you to the corner office or increasing your commission.

3. Don't take "no" for an answer. If your boss denies your request, ask him if he can help you understand the reasons for his response. Then ask if he would change his mind if those conditions improved. "Often you can set up a contingent raise, in which you'll get the money if you can help your department come in under budget or increase sales," says Ury.

4. Have a good reason. You're more likely to get a raise if you can explain to your boss exactly why you need the money. "Think about what you want the raise for—to pay for your kids' education, or simply to move up to the same pay level as a coworker," says Ury. "Then go in and make your case."

5. Know the industry standard. "In negotiating, no one—especially a boss—likes to get the sense that he's backing down," says Ury. To avoid that obstacle, back up your request with objective data. Find out the average salary for someone in your position at another company, or come up with a reasonable estimate of how much revenue you've generated for the company through sales, ideas or new products. "It's much easier for your boss to go with the standard than to meet your demands," says Ury. For info on standard salary figures, call the human resources departments at similar companies and ask for the salary range for a position equivalent to yours. If you get the runaround, contact your local office of the U.S. Department of Labor's Bureau of Labor Statistics, which keeps salary standards for many different industries. Or, check the reference section of your library for *The American Almanac of Jobs and Salaries* (Avon, 1993) to get more detailed descriptions of various occupations and their pay scales.

6. Order is important. Never go in and ask for more money without first telling your boss why you deserve it. "Once he says no to a figure, he probably won't reconsider, no matter how much explaining you do," says Ury.

7. Use percentages. "Absolute dollar values tend to make bosses nervous," says Ury. It's often better to talk about raises in terms of percentages and let him figure out the exact damage later.

8. Timing is everything. If you ask for a raise right before your boss starts working on the new budget, you're more likely to get it than if you wait until he's finished. You're also more likely to get a raise after you complete a major project or close a big sale.

9. Don't go to the well too often. "If you're asking for a raise more than once every 12 months, you're probably asking too often," says Ury.

10. Rehearse. Even the best negotiators can lose their bearings when the heat is on. To maximize your chances of staying cool, have your wife or buddy play your boss and try out your negotiating skills.

11. Write out your request. Once you discuss your proposal face-to-face with your boss, leave him a hard copy. Having it in writing proves to him that you've thought it through, and he can use the text as an outline when he goes to bat for you with the CEO. "You want to make it as easy as possible for him to say yes," says Ury.

12. Schedule an appointment. Never spring a raise request on your boss. Set up a time when you can state your case without interruptions. "Pay attention to your boss's typical stress level during the week and schedule your meeting for a time when he tends to be most relaxed and willing to listen," says Ury.

Becoming a Good Manager

Stephen R. Covey
Chairman of the Covey Leadership Center and author of *The 7 Habits of Highly Effective People* (Simon & Schuster, 1989)

1. Don't hire clones. "We all have the natural tendency to surround ourselves with people who think the same way we do," says Covey. Although they may be the best guys to take to a ball game, they don't make for the most effective staff. Build a complementary team in which your employees' strengths make up for your weaknesses.

2. Laissez-faire. When delegating a project to one of your employees, meet with him up front to discuss the project's goals and your vision of the outcome. Once you're on the same page, back off and let him come up with his own solutions. "If you make all the decisions for your staff and only let them turn the screwdrivers, you'll kill their morale—and their productivity," says Covey.

3. Pay your respects. "Even if there's no money in the budget for raises, there are lots of ways to keep your employees motivated," says Covey. Involving them in important decisions or challenging projects, recognizing them publicly for good work or simply upgrading their job titles are all inexpensive morale boosters that go a long way toward building employee devotion.

4. Build feedback loops. To increase the efficiency of the entire company, set up a system in which your employees get anonymous feedback from the people with whom they interface—inside and outside your department. For example, staff who deal with customers should get feedback from them; those in charge of billing should hear from the guys in accounts receivable. And above all, you should hear from everyone who works for you.

5. Develop an evaluation form. To give your employees the safety to express their concerns without fear of reprisal, develop a short, standardized form they can use to rate you (or other employees) on a scale of one to ten. Include criteria like "listening skills," "respect" and "morale building." Also, leave space for more specific comments.

6. Be humble. "To be a good boss you have to have humility," says Covey. "Think of your employees as customers, and every time you get the chance, ask them how you can help them."

7. Set up quarterly meetings. Meet with each of your employees at least three or four times a year to share with them your goals for the department and to give them an informal evaluation of their strengths and weaknesses. Not only will this make them feel like they have a say, but it also gives you the chance to point out areas in which you think they could boost their performance before the big year-end review.

8. Be a buffer. Just because *your* boss is on your back, that's no reason to get on the backs of your employees. In fact, when your employees see you staying cool under pressure, they're more likely to do the same.

9. Develop other interests. If your employees see you engaging in activities to develop your body and mind—like running on your lunch hour or attending a management training series—they'll have more respect for you than if you're just THE BOSS.

Saving for Retirement

David Chilton
Former stockbroker, president of Financial Awareness Corp. and author of *The Wealthy Barber: Everyone's Common-Sense Guide to Becoming Financially Independent* (Prima Publishing, 1991)

1. Have your company save for you. The least painful and most profitable way to save for retirement is to maximize your contribution to your company's 401(k) plan, or the similar 403 (b) if you work for a nonprofit agency. "You can't make a bigger financial mistake than to avoid these plans—especially if your company matches your investment," says Chilton.

2. Go global. If your company offers you a choice, have at least some of your 401(k) money invested in a global equity mutual fund that has a manager with a track record for success. "Concentrating your investment in one industry or country is a mistake," says Chilton.

3. Force yourself to save. If your company doesn't have a pension program, or you're self-employed, stick 10 percent of every check into a retirement account before you spend a cent. "Forced saving is what usually separates well-heeled retirees from the rest," says Chilton.

4. Get help when picking your own retirement plan. IRAs, Keoghs and SEPs all have their advantages and disadvantages. To determine the right one for your situation, it's best to talk things over with your accountant or a financial adviser at your bank.

5. List your spouse as your IRA beneficiary. Then, in the event of your death, your IRA can be rolled over into hers without any tax ramifications.

6. Contribute to your retirement plan early in the year. You have until April 15th of the following year to put your money into a retirement account and still deduct it. But contributing as early in the year as possible reduces the temptation to blow your money and increases the length of time it spends accumulating tax-deferred interest. "Contributing early, year after year, can mean tens of thousands of dollars in interest," says Chilton.

7. Start young. The real power behind saving for retirement is compound interest—in other words, making interest on interest you've already earned. So the earlier you start saving, the better. For example, two twenty-two-year-old twins decide to start saving for retirement. The first opens an IRA and invests $2,000 a year for six years, and then stops. The other brother waits till the seventh year to open his IRA and then contributes $2,000 a year for the next 37 years. Both earn a rate of 12 percent interest. At the age of 65, both will have the same amount in their accounts—$1,200,000.

8. Max out your 401(k) before going to tax-deferred annuities. While tax-deferred annuities allow your money to grow interest-free like a 401(k), you can't deduct your investment from your taxable income. To make matters worse, annuities have to be bought through salespeople who charge a commission. "Don't try to get too fancy," says Chilton. "Max out your 401(k) first, then check with your accountant to see if annuities are for you."

9. Keep your emergency fund realistic. "Many financial planners recommend keeping a readily available emergency fund equivalent to four-to-six months' gross income," says Chilton. "But I don't think it makes sense to have $10,000 or more sitting around earning fully taxable low rates of return. In most cases, a two- to three-thousand-dollar emergency fund is all you really need. If you fear an expensive emergency looms in your future, establish a $10,000 line of credit at your bank."

10. Send your kids to college on savings bonds. When used for education, the interest they earn is free of local, state and federal income tax. "That can make them hard to beat," says Chilton.

11. Beware of prepaid tuition programs. Unlike savings bonds, these programs—in which you pay a fixed sum over a number of years prior to your kid's enrollment—limits the schools he can attend and can leave you with a big tax bill down the road. "Most states will make you pay tax on the difference between what you prepaid for tuition and the actual costs when your child enrolls," says Chilton.

Starting Your Own Business

Stephen Harper
Director, The Small Business Institute at the University of North Carolina, Wilmington; author of *The McGraw-Hill Guide for Managing Growth in Your Emerging Business* (McGraw-Hill, 1994)

1. Look for customers in search of a business. One of the biggest mistakes entrepreneurs make is focusing on their own interests instead of the market's needs. "A business isn't a hobby," says Harper. "Don't sell pets just because you're a pet lover. Look for a need in the community, and fill it."

2. Don't try to be everything to everybody. "Focus your attention on a small group of your most loyal customers and give them exactly what they want," says Harper.

3. Attend a trade show. If you're thinking about opening a bookstore, for instance, join a trade association for retail booksellers and attend their annual conference. "It's amazing how much information people will give you about their business if you're not competing in the same town," says Harper.

4. Find free help. The U.S. Small Business Administration (listed under the United States Government section in the blue pages of your phone book) can be a virtual warehouse of information for prospective entrepreneurs.

Many universities also have business schools and small business development centers that can help you develop a business plan and advise you along the way. Some cities even have a Service Corps of Retired Executives (SCORE), which will give you inside info for free. Your local Small Business Administration chapter can tell you whether your town has a SCORE office. Or check with the reference department of your library.

5. Forget partnerships. Although bringing in a partner or two can be a quick way to raise capital, it's best to try and go it alone. "It's hard to get the right chemistry," says Harper. "And since you have unlimited liability among partners, the actions of one can cause all of you to go broke."

6. Have a 90-day financial security blanket. Since it usually takes a year to break even, many businesses fail because they are undercapitalized from the start. "Don't open your doors until you have enough money in the bank to pay all your expenses for 90 days," says Harper. "Otherwise, you risk dying on the vine."

7. Borrow from a bank that knows you. That maximizes your chances of getting start-up money. "A small bank may take a risk on you in the hope that you'll remember them as you grow and expand— a larger one might not," says Harper.

8. Have a plan. A well thought out business plan and market analysis will dramatically improve your chances of getting a loan. If you go to the bank with just an idea—no matter how good it is—you'll probably get shot down.

9. Have a specialist set up your books. Hiring an accountant who works with a number of small businesses will not only make bookkeeping easier—it can also keep you from being shut down. "If you miss your Social Security payment deadline, the government can lock you out of your own business," says Harper.

10. Take a bookkeeping or accounting course before you start. That way, you won't have to rely on your accountant for day-to-day tasks. Many community colleges offer business courses for prospective owners.

11. Incorporate immediately. Hiring a commercial attorney and filing articles of incorporation limits your own personal liability and makes it easier to sell your business, bring in a new owner or pass it on to your kids. "It also shows suppliers and customers you're serious about what you're doing," says Harper.

12. Time your opening. If you start a business early in the year, you may miss the cutoff date for listings in the Yellow Pages. That can devastate a young business, especially if you're not in a high-traffic location. In general, it's best to schedule your opening in the latter months of the year.

13. Plan for expansion. While it's best to start with a small store, select a location that has expansion opportunities. For example, if you're leasing space in a strip mall, ask to have a "first option on adjoining spaces" clause written into your lease. "It may cost you a bit more money up front," says Harper. "But if you're successful, the last thing you want to hurt you is a lack of space."

14. Be patient. Even if business is booming, wait two to three years before you expand. "The first couple of years are critical for a small business, and you don't want to do anything that's going to cost you a good chunk of change," says Harper.

How Ben & Jerry Did It
Ben Cohen
Cofounder, Ben & Jerry's, Inc.

1. *Befriend the community.* "The most important thing to realize is that there's a spiritual aspect to business. As you give, you receive; as your business supports the community, the community supports your business," says Cohen. An example of that is the "Pint-For-A-Pint" promotion. For a pint of blood, donors at local Red Cross blood drives receive a coupon for a free pint of Chunky Monkey—or any other flavor of their choice. "It's a great way to interact with great people,"says Cohen.

2. *Make it an experience, not an advertising gimmick.* "You can do all the fantastic marketing in the world, but if the customer is not getting a positive total experience, it's not going to work," says Cohen. "Early on, we did very little advertising—bumper stickers and ice cream samples, for the most part. People were attracted to the store because of the quality of the product and the quality of our service—that's what's always going to make the difference."

Playing the Stock Market

Peter Lynch
Creator of Fidelity Investment's billion-dollar Magellan Fund and author of the best-seller *Beating the Street* (Simon & Schuster, 1994) and *One Up on Wall Street* (Simon & Schuster, 1989)

1. Never buy on impulse. "Stocks aren't lottery tickets," says Lynch. "You have to get to know the company behind them." Before you buy, get a complete investor's packet and subscribe to a trade magazine that covers the industry. "If you can't explain to your kid in three minutes what a company does, you have no business buying its stock," says Lynch.

2. Don't worry about wasting time. "In the long run, giving yourself at least a few months to get to know a company is worth the risk of losing out on some of the company's growth," says Lynch.

"Even if you bought Wal-Mart stock 10 *years* after it went public, you still would have made 35 times your money."

3. Look at the balance sheet. Companies that have a lot of debt have a hard time surviving the ups and downs of the economy. "Never invest in a company without first making sure it doesn't have a pile of debt," says Lynch.

4. Concentrate your investments. "Realistically, you can only be an expert on six or seven companies at a time," says Lynch. Pick seven you're interested in, do your research and invest in the ones that are doing well and have healthy balance sheets. "You don't need many successes like Home Depot, Wal-Mart or Toys 'R' Us to make a fortune." On the other hand, if you do superficial research on 60 or 70 companies, you'll get superficial returns.

5. Buy what you know. When it comes to the field you work in, you have a big advantage over the professionals, who can't keep track of the developments in all the industries they invest in. "For example, if you're an auto dealer, you'll be one of the first to know whether you, or one of your competitors, is coming out with a top-notch vehicle," says Lynch. "So why would you want to go buy stock in, say, pharmaceuticals, about which you know next to nothing?"

6. Look in your backyard. Another advantage you have over institutional investors is that you can invest in local companies that you can follow easily.

7. Buy where you shop. "Malls are great places to do some of your investing research," says Lynch. "Chances are, if you love the store, you'll like the stock." But before you buy, don't forget to check the company's balance sheet for debt. Also, do some research to find out where it is in its life cycle. If the chain already has stores in all 50 states, there's probably not much more room for growth. However, if it's only in 10 or 12 states, it has lots of room to flourish.

8. Join a club. Investing clubs—in which each person is responsible for researching several companies and reporting back to the group—are a good way to diversify your stock holdings. "On average, investing clubs have a better record for beating the market than professionals," says Lynch. "Having to justify your investment choices to a group of people keeps you from taking too many risks." To find out more about starting an investment club, contact the not-for-profit National Association of Investors Corporation at (810) 583-6242.

9. Sink your surplus into stocks. "There was only one decade this century in which stocks didn't outperform both bonds and CDs," says Lynch. So when you're investing your extra capital, don't be lured by the interest income of bonds and CDs. It's better to buy stocks and sell some shares when you need cash.

10. Buy regularly. "Buying stock shouldn't be an emotional decision," says Lynch. Set up a schedule that allows you to make invest-

ments on a regular basis, "like you pay your health insurance premiums," he says. One exception: If a company has a major windfall—from the release of a successful product, for example—you may want to buy some extra shares on the spot.

11. Don't jump around. The surest recipe for investment disaster is to jump in and out of a company. In general, you should hold on to a stock for a year, if not longer. "My best returns came on companies I was with for five or six years," says Lynch.

12. Avoid options. Options—which gamble on how a company's stock will do in the next two to three months—are about the riskiest investments around. "What a stock does in 60 or 90 days is extremely random," says Lynch. "But what it does over the course of a couple years relates directly to how well the business is doing."

13. Be sure of a turnaround company. Don't buy a company's stock just because it fell to a new low and you think it's a bargain. "There's nothing that says it won't go to zero," says Lynch. When investing in a turnaround company, wait for the stock to start climbing again and check its balance sheet for debt. "If they don't have any debt, it's a good sign the company won't fail."

14. Forget about the market. "It would be very useful to know exactly what the economy is going to do before it happens," says Lynch. But since that's not possible, the best thing you can do is get to know a few companies and pick the strongest ones. "If a company is truly strong, both the ups and downs of the market will work in your favor, since you'll be able to pick up more shares when the price drops."

Beating a Tax Audit

Boyd Thomas, C.P.A.
Former IRS agent turned tax accountant

1. Answer only the questions you're asked. Auditors don't have the right to ask you about anything that isn't in your audit letter. "If you ramble on, you're likely to wind up owing more money," says Thomas.

2. Be professional. Don't expect any breaks if you go in with a chip on your shoulder and a shoe box full of receipts. "Most auditors are underpaid and overworked, so the smoother you make the audit, the better off you'll be," says Thomas.

3. Add up your receipts. Sure, the auditor will want to see all the pertinent receipts, but he probably won't want to add them up. When you go to the audit, bring the receipts and a calculator tape showing the total. Often the auditor will just glance over the tape and say OK.

4. Never contradict your form. "Always have a reasonable explanation ready to justify any deductions or expenses you may have inflated," says Thomas. "Even if they don't accept your story, admitting you cheated ruins your credibility for the rest of the audit."

5. Get help. Unless your audit letter questions only one or two figures on your form that you can easily clear up with receipts, it pays to hire a tax accountant to represent you. (Find one who's earned Enrolled Agent credentials from the U.S. Treasury Department.) Accountants often know the local auditors and can make negotiating easier, says Thomas.

6. Don't use cash. Canceled checks and credit card statements are your best receipts because you can easily get duplicates for an audit. It pays to have a separate checking account and credit card solely for business use.

7. Leave your bank statements and last year's tax form at home. "Even though the audit letter may tell you to bring them, most auditors use bank statements and old tax forms to fish for other problems," says Thomas. If the auditor persists, say you've lost them and need a few weeks to get copies; then call your tax accountant.

Buying a New Car

Robert Ellis
Manager, Car Bargains, the only nonprofit car-shopping service in the U.S.

1. Be informed. The only way to negotiate the best deal on a car is to know exactly how much the dealer paid for it and how much he's trying to make on you. To find out the figures, consult a new-car buying guide at a local bookstore—don't trust the invoice the dealer shows you. Add up the dealer's cost on the car and all the options (including tax, tags, delivery costs and advertising fees) and compare that to the dealer's bottom line. "The standard markup will differ among cars, but in general, if he's making more than $100 to $300 on a domestic car or $300 to $800 on an import— you're paying too much," says Ellis.

2. Figure everything. Before negotiating a price, make sure you include all the add-ons you want. "If you work out a great deal on the car up front and then let him tack on the extras like air conditioning, mud flaps, cruise control, floor mats and a CD player, you may end up paying too much," says Ellis.

3. Find out about rebates before you buy. Many dealers won't tell you about factory incentives or rebates so that they can pocket the money for themselves. To find out about such deals, call the manufacturers directly or look for the list of current promotions in the monthly *Car Deals* newsletter. Call (800) 475-7283 for a copy.

4. Foster competition. "If they feel there's no competition, dealers may try to gouge you," says Ellis. Tell the dealer up front that you're soliciting offers from two or three of his competitors—that encourages him to give you a good number on the first go-round. Then call other dealerships and ask if they can beat the first guy's deal. (If they refuse to make you an offer over the phone, call another dealership.) Making the dealers bid against each other can easily save you a thousand bucks.

5. Go out of town. When shopping for the best price over the phone, call the manufacturer and ask them for the names and phone numbers of all their dealers in a 50- to 100-mile radius of your home. "Any authorized dealer can service your car, so buying a car 50 miles from home doesn't mean you'll have to take it back there every time you need service," says Ellis.

6. Take a test drive. While it's a good idea to read up on the types of cars you're interested in, don't try to make a final decision without a test drive. No matter how good a deal you get, you wind up losing if you're not comfortable in the car or don't like the way it rides.

7. Don't fall for the "today-only special deal." That's just a gimmick to keep you from shopping around. Even if you think you've got a great deal, tell them you need some time to think about it, and then make a couple calls. "Ninety-nine times out of a hundred, you'll be able to get the same deal—or better—when you come back," says Ellis. And just in case you didn't already know, never leave a deposit until you're prepared to drive the car home.

8. Ask for the sales manager. To protect their commission, many car salesmen won't cut a tight deal, but the manager might.

9. Let hot cars cool. When a much-hyped car is first released, demand usually outpaces supply for four to six months. That makes it almost impossible to get a good price. "If you see only one on the lot, chances are you're going to pay too much," says Ellis.

10. Time your shopping. Your chances of getting a rebate or an incentive are much higher at the end of a model year, when dealers are trying to make room for the new models. In the past, most new models were introduced in September, but now manufacturers stagger the release of their various models throughout the year. To find out when the model year on a car is up, contact the manufacturer.

11. Dicker with the sticker. With the exception of Saturn, almost all dealerships will budge on their no-dicker sticker prices—if you negotiate.

12. Make one deal at a time. In most cases, you'll do better if you sell your old car outright before buying a new one. But if you've decided to trade it in, don't tell the salesman until after he's written down his best deal on the one he's trying to sell you. "If you try to make both deals simultaneously, you're going to lose money somewhere," says Ellis. Compare the dealer's offer for your car with the blue-book value your bank gives you. If it's within $200, it's worth taking. If not, shop your clunker around at other dealerships—one may buy it outright from you.

13. Know when to lease. The mileage and wear-and-tear clauses can wind up costing you a lot of money if you hold on to a car for too long. If you plan on keeping the car for more than three years, it's best to buy it. However, if you're going to be switching sooner, a lease is usually better.

14. Be patient. Getting a good deal takes at least a week's worth of research and shopping. If you're not willing to put in the time, using a car-buying service or broker can save you money. For an up-front fee, the service will negotiate with the dealer of your choice for you. Brokers, on the other hand, buy the cars first and deliver them to you. In head-to-head comparisons, the car-buying services—which usually charge around $150 to $200—provide the best deal.

Buying a Used Car

Ray Magliozzi
cohost of "Car Talk" on National Public Radio and coauthor of *Car Talk* (Dell, 1991)

1. Older cars with less mileage are better than younger cars with more mileage. "I'd buy a seven-year-old car with 20,000 miles before I'd buy a two-year-old car with 70,000," says Magliozzi. "Mileage, not age, wears a car down."

2. Never buy a used sports car, 4 × 4 or pickup truck. These vehicles are worked hard, so unless you know for sure the owner handled it gently, it's best to buy one new.

3. Eyeball the owner. "If he's a pencil-necked geek who has every shovel in his garage on the right hook, chances are he takes good care of his car," says Magliozzi. "Accountant- and engineer-types are good car owners. Salesmen are the worst."

4. Older owners are better, too. "People over 30 have more respect for everything, including their cars," says Magliozzi. "Never buy from someone who is under age 30."

5. Look at the title. All cars have a paper trail documenting the previous

owners. If a car has more than one previous owner, don't buy it.

6. Buy a rental, not a lease. Rental cars are usually well maintained, while leased cars are usually "beaten to an untimely death," says Magliozzi. You can buy a rental from most small rental companies, but national carriers are required to return them to the manufacturer, who redistributes them to dealerships for resale. If a dealer says his car came from a rental agency, ask to see the paperwork.

7. Get a feel for it. "Comfort is one of the most important things about a car," says Magliozzi. "If the car's geometry doesn't fit yours, don't buy it."

8. Ask your mechanic. "Most mechanics specialize now, and if your favorite service guy won't work on the car—or can't refer you to someone reliable who can—you probably don't want to buy it," says Magliozzi. If your mechanic will service the car, ask him to assess everything that's wrong with it *and* everything that he thinks will go wrong. Get an estimate for repairs and consider that in the price.

9. Don't be fooled by the "garage-kept" description. Cars that were kept in a garage aren't necessarily in better condition than ones that weren't. "A heated garage actually speeds up the rusting process," says Magliozzi.

10. Be patient. "You can't buy a good car in a weekend," says Magliozzi. Give yourself four to six weeks to do a thorough job and get the best deal.

Paying Less in Taxes

Kevin McCormally
Tax editor, *Kiplinger's Personal Finance Magazine*, and author of
Kiplinger's Sure Ways to Cut Your Taxes (Kiplinger's, 1995)

1. Recognize you can pay less. "Tax planning isn't only for fat cats," says McCormally. "Most people in the country pay too much tax because they don't take advantage of simple tax planning strategies."

2. Max out your IRA. "Most Americans can still deduct their contributions to individual retirement accounts," says McCormally. So whether you work for someone else or you're self-employed, stashing $2,000 a year—the maximum tax-free contribution—into an IRA is the easiest tax break around. "If you're in the 28 percent tax bracket, a $2,000 deductible automatically saves you $560 in taxes, and the money in the account grows tax-deferred until you withdraw it."

3. Take all your deductions. "Not taking a deduction you deserve for fear of being audited is the equivalent of paying protection to the IRS," says McCormally.

4. Keep track of your investments. "Many people overpay the tax on their stocks and mutual funds because they don't keep accurate records," says McCormally. The biggest mistake is paying tax twice on reinvested dividends. Here's an example: Say you buy $1,000 worth of stock. Then you reinvest $100 of the dividends to buy more shares before selling the whole lot a year later for $1,200. Your reported gain should be only $100, not $200. "You paid tax on the dividend the year it was paid to you," says McCormally. "If you count it as part of your gain, you'll pay tax on it again when you sell."

5. Do it yourself, if you can. If you have a fairly simple financial situation, you're better off filing your return on your own or using a computerized tax preparation kit than paying an accountant to do the job. But if you have a number of investments, run a side business, bought or sold a home or inherited a significant amount of property, paying an accountant to help you is usually a money- saving investment.

6. Know when to itemize. For most people, taking the standard deduction is usually a better deal moneywise—and timewise—than itemizing their deductions. But if you think itemizing will save you money, add up the three major deductible expenses: home mortgage interest, state income taxes and charitable contributions. If the total falls within $200 of your standard deduction, talk to an accountant about itemizing—it will probably save you money.

7. Use an employer reimbursement account for medical and child-care expenses. Offered by many companies as a fringe benefit, these accounts are one of the best tax breaks around. Here's how they work: Each year, designate the amount of pretax money you want transferred directly from your paycheck to the account. Then after you pay a child-care or medical bill, submit it to your employer for reimbursement from the account. "This system lets you pay your health and child-care bills with tax-exempt money," says McCormally. One drawback: Leftover money is not refunded to you or carried over to the next year. "But it's such a big tax break you can forfeit one-third of the money and still come out ahead," says McCormally. Better yet, use excess funds for a new pair of glasses or a checkup.

8. Deduct your points. In the past, only buyers could deduct the points they paid to get a mortgage on their principal residence. But, if you as the buyer convinced the seller to pay all or part of the points for you, no one got the deduction. Now, in almost all cases, the buyer gets to deduct the points, even if the seller paid them. "Since each point represents one percent of the mortgage amount, this can very quickly become a big-buck item," says McCormally.

9. Invest in tax-free bonds. While they have lower yields than most corporate bonds, tax-free bonds may actually be more lucrative. Say you're in the 31 percent tax bracket, and you're trying to choose between a tax-free bond with a 7 percent yield and a taxable bond with a 10.14 percent yield. Use this simple formula to see how they compare: Subtract your tax bracket from 1 (1 − 0.31 = .69). Then divide the tax-free yield by that number: (.07 / .69 = .1014). If you multiply your answer by 100, you'll get the percentage yield you'd need on a taxable bond to match the tax-free yield (.1014 × 100 = 10.14 percent). "In this case, you get the same return on the tax-free bond as the taxable bond," says McCormally. "And if the tax-free bond also escapes state income taxes, you'll come out ahead."

10. Educate your kids on tax-free savings bonds. "People typically think of these as lousy investments," says

McCormally. "But if you use them to put your kids through college, they can be free of state and federal income tax. That often makes them a good investment," says McCormally.

11. Don't overpay any inheritance tax. Unknown to most people, there's a tax break that forgives the levy on any profit that has built up in stocks, real estate or other assets when the owner dies. Say, for example, that you inherit stock that your father bought for $1,000 and that was worth $10,000 when he died. When you sell the stock, your base for figuring taxable gain or loss is that $10,000 date-of-death value. So, if you sell the stock for $9,000, you actually have a $1,000 tax-deductible loss—even though you've got $9,000 in your pocket, says McCormally.

12. Know the rules—even if you use an accountant. "Your accountant is only as good as the information you give him—the more you know, the more he can do for you," says McCormally. Most community colleges offer basic tax courses and many tax preparation offices give low-cost seminars to help you brush up. Or you can pick up an up-to-date tax preparation book at your local bookstore.

13. Cut your withholding. If your typical refund is more than $1,000, you're letting Uncle Sam use money that could be earning you interest. To keep the government from taking more out of your check than it has the right to, simply ask your employer to add more allowances to your W-4 form. "For each withholding allowance you add, you'll get $50 to $60 extra in your monthly paycheck," says McCormally. For a rough estimate on how many allowances to add, divide your refund by $700 (if you're in the 28 to 31 percent tax bracket) and round to the nearest whole number.

Buying a House

Peter G. Miller
Author of numerous real estate books, including *Successful Real Estate Negotiation* (HarperCollins, 1994) and *The Common-Sense Mortgage* (HarperCollins, 1994)

1. See what you can afford. Before you look at any houses, go to several lenders (banks, mortgage banks, savings and loan associations, credit unions) to see how much of a mortgage you qualify for. "That'll keep you from wasting time on properties that are out of your league," says Miller.

2. Keep shopping. Mortgage rates change just about every day, so the key to getting a good deal is to check with as many lenders as you can, as often as you can.

3. It doesn't have to be your first house to qualify for "first-time buyer" assistance. "As long as you haven't owned any real estate in the past three years, you'll usually qualify," says Miller.

4. Have a plan when applying for financing. If you're going to be in a house less than ten years, it's usually cheaper to take zero points (or as few as possible) and get a higher interest rate. However, if you plan on staying longer, it's better to take the points and pay a lower interest rate. "Never buy a house without having someone run the numbers both ways to show you which would be cheaper," says Miller.

5. Over the short term, it's better to rent than buy. "If you're only going to keep a house for three or four years, you're not likely to make up all your costs and sell the house for a profit," says Miller.

6. Assemble a team. You need at least four people to help you buy a house: a buyer/broker to find suitable properties, an attorney to check over the offer before you sign, a structural inspector to assess the house's soundness and an accountant to show you how the purchase will affect your tax situation. "It may cost you a few hundred bucks," says Miller. "But for the price of a set of drapes, you can buy a house the right way and not have to worry about things popping up down the road."

7. Make sure you'll get your deposit back. Whenever you put money down on a house, make sure you sign an agreement that the money is totally refundable if the deal goes sour.

8. Don't give the seller the home-field advantage. Savvy sellers often draw up their own contracts and call them "official." While there's nothing illegal about it, signing a personalized contract will most often leave you holding the short end of the stick. Have a real estate lawyer explain each clause and make any necessary changes.

9. Beware of quitclaim deeds. Many shady sellers use quitclaim deeds—which in effect say, "Whatever I have, I give you"—to sell a house they don't own or that has debts remaining to be paid on it. "Never buy property with a quitclaim deed without doing a title search at a local courthouse and consulting with a real estate attorney first," says Miller.

10. Never accept oral promises. "They're basically worthless," says Miller. If you really want the seller to come back and finish up the shed after you've moved in, have him put it in writing.

11. Be specific. "If you write into the contract that the house should come with a washer and dryer, specify the exact make and model," says Miller. "You may be thinking of a brand-new mechanical marvel and end up with a washboard and clothesline."

12. Watch out for merger. Once you close on a house, the sales contract is automatically "merged" into the deed—unless the agreement says otherwise—and it no longer exists in the eyes of the courts, says Miller. That can make it difficult to have the seller complete all the improvements he promised to make. To assure that the work gets done, have the contract stipulate that the seller will set up an escrow account at the time of closing to cover any work he hasn't completed. If he's going to do the work himself, have him set aside a reasonable amount and agree to return it to him when the job's done.

13. Get a "good faith" estimate of the closing costs. Closing a deal on a house can cost you thousands of dollars in taxes and professional fees, says Miller. "You can't always get the exact numbers up front, but having a ballpark figure before you make your offer can help you avoid any major surprises. And you can usually get the seller to pick up part of the closing tab."

14. Set limits on an adjustable rate mortgage. To minimize the risks of an adjustable rate mortgage (ARM)—a home loan with a fluctuating interest rate—make sure the mortgage papers clearly state the following information: the maximum interest rate you are willing to pay over the life of the loan, the maximum annual interest increase allowed each year and the maximum monthly payment increase.

15. Look for ARMs with the least risk. "Lenders use a variety of financial indexes on which to base their rates," says Miller. Indexes that cover a longer span of events, like the 11th District Cost of Funds Index (COFI) or one-year U.S. Treasury bonds,

change more gradually than most other indexes—and can keep your rates fairly stable.

16. Check out hybrid ARMs. These mortgages, which carry a fixed interest rate for 7 to 10 years before switching over to a variable rate, are usually good if you plan to sell your new house after a few years. The reason: You'll typically get a lower interest rate than with a fixed-rate loan, but you'll be out before the variable interest kicks in. But just in case you decide to stay, treat a hybrid like a traditional ARM and have limits put on the interest before you sign.

HOW TO MAKE A STRUCTURAL INSPECTION
Bob Vila

*Host of "Bob Vila's Home Again" and author of numerous home improvement books,
including* Bob Vila's Tool Box *(Wm. Morrow, 1993) and*
Bob Vila's Workshop *(Wm. Morrow, 1994)*

1. *Make sure it's straight.* " 'Plumb' and 'level' are two of the most important words to keep in mind when you're looking at a house," says Vila. Even after the house has "settled," the ridge of the roof should be even with the horizon and the corners should meet neatly. If they're off, either the foundation has shifted or the wood on top of it is rotting.

2. *Look in the basement.* Water stains on the walls or ceiling of the cellar are also evidence of leakage and possibly rotting wood.

3. *Check the furnace and air conditioner.* "If they've been well maintained on the inside, they'll look it from the outside," says Vila. To confirm any suspicions you may have, ask the owners for maintenance receipts and copies of monthly bills. If the systems don't meet your standards—but you like the rest of the house—use them as bargaining chips to lower the price.

4. *Eye up the roof.* Use a pair of binoculars to look for missing shingles or black tar showing through worn-out colored shingles. Also, check around the chimney. If you can see the metal flashing, or there's a thick layer of tar covering it up, chances are there was a water leak that had to be repaired.

5. Check the plumbing and the electrical system. "Flush all the toilets, turn on all the faucets, make sure the drains work quickly and turn on all the lights," says Vila. Inspect the electrical box, too. If it uses screw-in fuses instead of switches, chances are there aren't enough outlets in the house and you'll have to have it rewired. "Once again, these are all bargaining chips," says Vila.

6. Save the new wallpaper for later. "The biggest mistake people make when buying an older home is to spend money trying to make it look nice before getting the plumbing, electrical and heating systems in perfect shape," says Vila. "After buying a new home, it's easy to lose sight of the fact that its primary function is to provide shelter."

7. Have a housing inspector look at the house before you make an offer. "While you might be able to identify most of the major problems yourself, someone who does it for a living will always find something you've missed," says Vila. (Once again, use any shortcomings as bargaining chips during the final deal.) To find a good inspector, never take the seller's recommendation.. Instead, ask your bank lending officer for some suggestions.

Selling Your House

William G. Effros
Author, *How to Sell Your Home in 5 Days* (Workman Publishing, 1993)

1. Start low and hold an auction to drive up the price. "Most people list the highest price they think they can get and work down from there," says Effros. But that strategy often turns prospective buyers away before they even see the house. Instead, list the *lowest* you'd accept. Then hold an auction for interested parties, with your minimum price as the starting bid. The competition between bidders will drive up the price, says Effros.

2. Run a good ad. Advertisements that result in quick sales at the highest possible prices include a brief description of the house's highlights, a low price with an indication you're willing to bargain, a date for an open house and a line that creates a sense of urgency to get people to look at your house first. Your ad should run in major newspapers from Wednesday to Sunday. Here's a blueprint:

NORTH ANYTOWN   BY OWNER
5BR House on Pond   Deck   Patio
Den w/fpl   Din Rm   Liv Rm   3 Baths
$99,500 or Best Reasonable Offer
Inspection Sat.–Sun. 10–5
Home will be sold by Sunday Night to
Highest Bidder
(608) 555-3138

3. If you don't get 25 calls by Friday, your price is too high. Yank the ad and relist it at a lower price next week. "The system works on the premise that you'll get a total of 100 calls and at least 40 will show up to look," says Effros. "The more competition you can bring in, the more money you'll get for your house."

4. Set the price below a "magic number." If you list your house at a round figure like $155,000 or $120,000, people are more likely to think that you won't budge on it, says Effros. Instead, set it just below the "magic number," at $149,500, for example. "People may think you'll go as low as $140,000."

5. Skip the appraisals. "Let the market determine the price of your house, not one guy with a bunch of charts," says Effros.

6. And the broker. "Brokers have a conflict of interest," says Effros. "They want to list your house at a price that ensures they get their commission, not at one that ensures you'll get the most for your house."

7. Be honest. Show prospective buyers the complete home inspection report, tell them *everything* that is wrong with the house, and say they are bidding on an "as is" basis. "Not only will you sleep easier, but you want to give people the feeling they're bidding against other prospective buyers, not against you," says Effros.

8. Wage a price war. During the open house, place a bidding sheet on a table near the entrance where people can write down their name, phone number and bid. Then on Sunday night—between 5 and 8 P.M., after the open house is over—begin a round-robin bidding procedure over the telephone. First, call the highest bidder. Tell him he has made the top offer and ask him if he'd like to up it any before you call the others. Then call the next highest bidder to see if he can beat the top bid. Go through as many rounds as necessary until there's only one bidder left.

9. Explain the bidding process. Give people a quick rundown when they call for directions to the open house and post a clear description next to the bidding sheet.

10. Get an attorney. Each state has its own laws governing real estate sales and auctions, so contact an attorney before you list your ad. Also, once the sale is made, it's necessary to have an attorney qualify the buyer and keep him from pulling a fast one.

11. Don't hold off till spring. The sooner you can sell your house, the better—even if you anticipate that the market may take a bit of an upswing in a year. "Every day you hold on to it, you have to pay more mortgage interest, taxes and repair bills," says Effros. "The only bad times to try to sell a house are over holidays and three-day weekends, when people stay home with their families," he says.

Getting Good Airline Fares

Ed Perkins
Editor, *Consumer Reports Travel Letter*

1. Develop a relationship with a travel agent. If a travel agent doesn't know you, chances are you'll get one of the first fares that pops up on his screen. "Find a hardworking agent and stick with him," says Perkins. "Once the agent gets to know you, he's more likely to take the extra time to scan the system for small carriers and different routes—where you often find the best deals."

2. Always ask agents to check smaller airlines. Many travel agents look only at the major carriers, but smaller carriers like Carnival, Kiwi, Midway, ValuJet and American Trans Air are also in the system and can offer great deals on domestic flights. "Assuming you'll al-ways get the best deal on a huge airline is a huge mistake," says Perkins.

3. Don't do it yourself. "It would take you half a day to call all the airlines out there to find the best price," says Perkins. "With their computers, travel agents can do the same search in seconds."

4. Look for a rebate agency. Airlines typically pay travel agents an 8 to 12 percent commission on every ticket they sell. However, to make their prices more attractive, some travel agencies sacrifice part of their commissions, giving customers 5 to 6 percent rebates on ticket prices. A few of the major rebate agencies are: Travel Avenue in Chicago,

(800) 333-3335; The Smart Traveller in Coconut Grove, Fla., (800) 448-3338; and Pennsylvania Travel in Paoli, Pa., (800) 331-0947. Rebate ticketing is also available through many credit cards—including gas cards—and Price Club and Costco discount stores.

5. Check the surrounding area. When a big city has two airports, it's not unusual for airlines to have very different fares, especially if one of the airports has competition among big and small carriers. Likewise, it may be significantly cheaper to fly into a neighboring city and rent a car or take a shuttle—particularly if you're traveling with your family or with a group. "Shopping around doesn't always work, but it's foolish not to check before you go," says Perkins.

6. Look for a stopover. You can often get big savings by stopping over in a city that's running special fares. For example, a round-trip ticket with no advance purchase from Dallas–Fort Worth Airport (DFW) to Tampa might cost $410 each way. But if you purchase a ticket from Dallas to New Orleans for $79 and then buy a ticket from New Orleans to Tampa for $99, you pay only $178 each way. Since these special offers usually last for only a few weeks, keep an eye on ads in your local paper to see what airlines are running specials through which airports. If you can work the discount city into your route, chances are you can save money.

7. Split two round-trips. Business travelers often have to pay high fares because they don't incorporate a Saturday night stay into their plans. However, many travelers who fly into the same destination more than once in a 30-day period save money by buying two round-trips and splitting the tickets. Here's how it works: Say you're making two Dallas-Boston round-trips this month, both without Saturday night stays. Each trip would cost $1,228 (a total of $2,456). To take advantage of the price breaks for Saturday night stays, book your first round-trip Dallas/Boston/Dallas. The Dallas-Boston leg should be dated for the start of your first trip. Date the Boston-Dallas leg for the return of your *second* trip. Book your second round-trip Boston/Dallas/Boston, dating the Boston-Dallas leg as the return of your first trip and the Dallas-Boston leg for the outbound part of your second trip. Each round-trip would cost you $574 (a total of $1,148 for two). That's a savings of $1,308 on the whole deal. "Some airlines have tried to label this procedure as fraudulent, but they've yet to prove it and they've just about given up trying to catch ticket splitters," says Perkins.

8. Buy the package. "When going overseas or to a beach destination, you'll usually save money by getting a package deal that includes airfare, hotel and maybe some meals," says Perkins.

9. Take a charter to the beach or Vegas. Many charter operators, like Wings of the World and MLT Vacation, run cheap flights between major cities and popular tourist centers. Since they're not in a travel agent's computer, the best way to find out about special charter deals is to watch the small ads in the travel section of your newspaper or call the charter operator directly. Two warnings: Charter flights are usually very crowded. And if you need to return early, you'll wind up paying full fare on a regular airline, since there are usually few backup flights on a charter.

10. To go overseas cheap, try a consolidator. To ensure they fill a certain portion of each plane, many major carriers sell some of their tickets through consolidators or discount travel agents at very low prices. "You'll almost always save a couple hundred bucks to Asia, and it's a great way to get tickets to Europe during the summer, when all the best fares are snatched up early," says Perkins. "But unfortunately, consolidators rarely offer deals on domestic flights." You can usually find consolidators' ads in the travel section of major newspapers.

11. Hitch a ride. AirHitch in New York, (212) 864-2000, serves as an unofficial standby agent for several international charter airlines. "None of the charters will admit to having standby seats available," says Perkins. But if you contact AirHitch, and don't mind hanging out at the airport for a few hours, you can wind up flying from New York to Europe for under $350 round-trip without advance notice.

12. Use your seniority. Most of the major domestic carriers offer discount flight coupons to people 62 and over. Each coupon costs about $140 to $150 (one way) and is good for almost any one-way domestic ticket the carrier offers. There are two drawbacks, however: The coupons come in blocks of four or eight and must be used within one year. And for shorter flights, you can usually get cheaper rates on low-fare airlines like Southwest.

13. Know the market. *Consumer Reports Travel Letter*, (800) 234-1970, and *Best Fares Discount Travel Magazine*, (800) 880-1234, keep track of all the latest deals offered by the airlines and can help you find bargains.

SPORTS

Arm Wrestling

Andy "The Cobra" Rhodes
Fourteen-time world champion in weight classes ranging from
165 to 190 pounds. Went 5,000–0 during a three-month stretch in
1992.

1. Be explosive. The average match is over in only a few seconds, so to win you have to strike fast. "Getting the jump will win you 95 percent of your matches," says Rhodes. "Hit hard and pull like crazy."

2. Pull, don't push. "The closer your arm is to your body the more leverage you'll have," says Rhodes. When wrestling with your right arm, *pull* your opponent's hand toward your left shoulder—don't try to push it straight over to the side.

3. Use a curl. Arm-wrestling contestants must line up with their wrists straight. But once the match begins, you can curl yours as much as you want. "Curling your wrist opens your opponent's," says Rhodes. "The more you do that, the better your chances of coming out on top."

4. Stay high. Gripping high on your opponent's thumb will give you more leverage.

5. Dig in. To get the strongest grip possible, dig your fingers into your opponent's hand like a vise. "Try to put your fingers through the back of his hand and into your own palm," says Rhodes (only half-jokingly).

6. Hit him with "the cobra." Rhodes credits his success, and nickname, to the technique he developed. As soon as the start command is given, pull your hand (and your opponent's) back to your nose, roll your wrist toward your body and drive your thumb to the corner of the table nearest your opposite shoulder. "When you do it right, you're virtually unbeatable," he says.

Bass Fishing

Shaw Grigsby
Professional bass fisherman, ranked fourth on BASS Fishing's all-time money winnings list

1. Fish early and late. It's easiest to catch bass one to two hours after daybreak and one to two hours before nightfall—their natural feeding times. And the low-light conditions of dusk and dawn make your lures harder to distinguish from the real thing.

2. Fish undercover. Bass like to hide in the shadows to ambush their prey. So instead of casting your line as far out into the water as you can, as many beginners do, fish around poles, stumps and docks. The best strategy is to throw your bait out past the shady side of an obstacle and work it back. "If you throw your bait too close to your target, you'll spook the fish," says Grigsby.

3. Be a depth finder. In the summer and winter, bass usually retreat to deeper water, so deep baits—like jigs, spoons or plastic worms—work best. But in the spring and fall, bass stay in the shallow water and you'll have more luck with worms, spinners, or buzz baits, which ride closer to the surface.

4. When in doubt, use a worm. "Dark red, purple or black plastic worms are the best all-around bass baits," says Grigsby. "They can catch a bass just about anytime and anyplace."

5. Be sensitive. Graphite rods are much more sensitive to strikes than fiberglass models. "A six- to seven-foot-long, medium-action graphite model is the best all-around bass fishing rod," says Grigsby.

6. Stay loose. The tighter you hold the rod, the less likely you are to detect the small bites that tell you where the fish are. Hold the rod as if it were made of glass.

7. Practice casting. Since bass like to hide around obstacles, good casters have a big advantage in bass fishing. "If you can't hit a washtub in your backyard at 25 feet, you aren't going to catch many bass," says Grigsby.

8. Cover your trail. Fish have a sense of smell, so leaving your scent on a lure can significantly reduce your chances of a good catch. To improve your odds, spray your lures with special scents you can get at most tackle stores. "Crawfish and shad scents work best because that's what bass like to eat," says Grigsby.

Bowling

Earl Anthony
Member, Professional Bowling Association Hall of Fame, and
record holder for winning the most major tournaments—45

1. Don't whip it. "If you throw the ball as hard as you can, the pins will scatter wildly instead of mixing with each other—leaving you with splits and other hard-to-make spares," says Anthony. "Control the ball and *roll* it down the lane."

2. Watch the arrows, not the pins. A common beginner's mistake is to watch the pins as you make your approach. But since the arrows on the lane are 45 feet closer, it's better to focus on them. "The closer you are to your target, the easier it is to hit it," says Anthony.

3. Don't throw the ball straight down the lane. "The more angle your ball has on it when it enters the pocket, the less it will deflect off the pins and the more likely you are to get a strike," says Anthony. If you're right-handed, roll the ball over the second arrow from the right toward the pocket. That will give you the greatest angle without putting the ball in the gutter. If you're a southpaw, aim for the second arrow from the left.

4. Start off-center. If you're right-handed, it's best to start your approach slightly to the right of center and walk toward the second arrow on a line to the pocket. Lefties should do the opposite.

5. Bowl like clockwork. As you bring the ball forward to release it, your arm should swing like a pendulum from your shoulder. "If you have to twist your arm or your wrist to get the ball to go toward the pocket, there's something wrong with your approach," says Anthony.

6. Only throw a hook if you're serious. Throwing a hook—by rotating your wrist slightly during the release—can significantly increase the angle at which your ball hits the pins and boost your score. But it can also make you wild. "If you're only bowling once a week, a hook's likely to make you inconsistent and drop your pin count," says Anthony.

7. Walk, don't run. Running up to the foul line may give you more mo-mentum, but it destroys your accuracy. "If you're not balanced when you release the ball, you'll never be a good bowler," says Anthony.

8. Have a towel handy. When you pick up the ball, oil from the lanes can get on your hands and compromise your grip. "You shouldn't have to squeeze your fingers inside the ball to keep it from slipping off your hand," says Anthony. If you forgot your towel, pick up your ball off the return by putting your fingers in the holes.

9. Get the angle on spares. Once again, the more angle you can get on the pins, the better your chances of flattening them. "For anything on the right of the lane, start your approach to the left. For anything on the left, start to the right," says Anthony. "Then walk toward the pins and fire at the arrow that completes the diagonal between you and them."

Softball

Bruce "The Bruiser" Meade
World record holder, longest home run in softball history
(510 feet)

1. Stay relaxed. Tightening your upper body and trying to kill the ball steals your power and is more likely to produce pop-ups than home runs. "If you stay loose and drive through the ball with your legs and midsection, you'll be able to hit the ball a ton," says Meade. "White knuckles mean you're too tense."

2. Stretch. A quick turn of the hips is essential for producing power. And the looser your hips are, the faster you can turn them. Stretch your legs and hips thoroughly before every game and for at least a few minutes on off days.

3. Keep your weight back. As you step into the ball, don't put all your weight onto your front foot. Instead, plant your foot and then explosively turn your back hip into it. "It's the hip torque that transfers power up from your feet, through to your legs and midsection and into your upper body and arms," says Meade.

4. Lift. "Going to the gym won't turn a bad hitter into a good one, but it can make a good hitter great," says Meade. To maximize your efforts, focus on your legs, backside and midsection. Then throw in some work for your upper back, chest and shoulders. "I do 6 to 8 reps per set, going slow on the way down and exploding as I push the weight up," he says.

5. Split the season. Lifting hard during the season will leave your muscles too fatigued to play their best. Build your strength in the off-season. Then during the in-season, cut your program nearly in half so that you're doing just enough to maintain your strength—without maxing out.

6. Don't try to launch it. Swinging straight up on the ball is the best way to hit pop-ups, not home runs. To get the most distance, swing up at a 45-degree angle. "It should feel just slightly upward," says Meade. Your position in the batter's box can help you develop the perfect swing. If you're facing a pitcher who throws flat, move up in the box to get the ball before it drops. If he's throwing a rainbow, move back so you can hit the ball as it starts to level out in front of you.

7. Buy light. You may think swinging a big stick makes you more macho. But a light bat that has a bit of weight at the end generates more speed and power than a heavier one. "I'm 6'6", 250 pounds and I use a 29-ounce bat with a 6-ounce plug," says Meade.

8. Invest in technology. Although they're expensive, bats made from high-tech materials allow you to hit the ball farther than traditional aluminum bats. "A CU-31 alloy bat may run you an extra 50 bucks, but it'll give you 15 to 25 more feet on each hit," says Meade.

9. Go long. The longer the bat the more leverage you'll have on the ball, so use the longest one possible—a 34-incher.

10. Leverage yourself. "By holding the bat high up in your hand you can turn a 34-inch stick into a 35-incher," says Meade. "It might not sound like much, but the extra leverage will add 30 feet to your ball." Here's how to do it: If you're a right-handed batter, grab the bat so that the ring finger of your left hand is wrapped around the knob at the bat's base and your middle finger is curled around the handle just above it. At this point, the knob should be sitting just below the midline of your palm with your pinky tucked underneath it. Lay your thumb across your middle finger and wrap your index finger around the tip of your thumb. (For extra gripping power, you can wrap some medical tape over the bottom inch and a half of the handle.) Your right hand should assume a normal grip just above your left hand. "It may feel a bit loose at first, but it works," says Meade.

11. Get cleats. Your legs generate much of your hitting power, so good footing is essential for monster shots. Running or basketball shoes don't have the traction you need and can significantly sap your strength.

Flag Football

Bob Butara
Quarterback, Gibb's flag football team of Cleveland, Ohio, winner of 11 national titles and one world championship

1. Throw short. Since flag football is played without the two tackles, quarterbacks have less time to set up and look for deep receivers. "Screens and five-yard slants over the middle work well," says Butara. Another of his favorite plays: Send five receivers out five to seven yards, and have them all hook away from the guys covering them.

2. Don't run. "Blocking is limited in flag football, so you're not going to win running the ball," says Butara. "We pass 99.9 percent of the time, and only run when there's a big hole."

3. Don't be a mad bomber. "You can't throw the bomb anytime you want—you have to use short passes to set up the deep stuff," says Butara. "When you see the defense move up to cover the short game, that's the time to go long."

4. Get a center with a good arm. "We run all our plays from the shotgun," says Butara. "By taking the snap 10 to 15 yards deep, I get an extra five seconds to read the defense and find a receiver." But drop back only half as far on short-yardage plays and when you're inside your opponent's 10. That way, you can get the pigskin to your receivers more quickly.

5. Spread it around. Throwing the ball to many different receivers, à la the San Francisco 49ers, will keep the defense guessing and increase your chances of marching down the field. However, if you find a weakness in your opponent's D, keep throwing at it until they find a way to stop you. "Sometimes I'll run the same play four times in a row," says Butara.

6. You got four downs, use 'em. "Aggressiveness is the difference between a great team and a good one," says Butara. "We go on fourth down 90 percent of the time, even on our own end of the field. The only time we'll punt is if we're pinned inside the 10."

7. Blitz. The most effective defense in touch football is one that puts constant pressure on the quarterback. "Always send one more guy than they're using to block," says Butara.

8. Stay in your lane. When rushing the quarterback, it's essential for defensive players to stay in their rushing lanes and contain the QB. "If the quarterback gets outside the pocket, he can wreak havoc on your secondary," says Butara. "Not only does he have five extra seconds to find a receiver, but he can tuck the ball under his arm and take off."

9. Go zone. With a constant blitz, it's easy to get burned on man-to-man defense, so it's best to use a zone secondary.

10. Spin. Spinning away from a would-be flag grabber is the surest way to make him miss.

11. Practice grabbing flags. Ripping the flags off a wide receiver with a full head of steam is like trying to sip a soda while four-wheeling. Set aside 10 or 15 minutes during each practice to work on your technique.

Running

Frank Shorter
Gold medalist, 1972 Olympic marathon; silver medalist, 1976 Olympic marathon

1. Go long. If you're training for a 5K or 10K, one of your weekly runs should be at least 1 hour long to build your endurance and teach your body to burn fat more efficiently. If you're training for a marathon, you'll need to do at least eight runs, each one lasting more than 1 hour and 15 minutes in the three months before your race. Three to four of those should be 20-milers. To stave off injury, do your long runs at a slow pace and don't run the next day.

2. Do interval training once or twice a week. "After about a year of running 20 miles a week, your speed will level off," says Shorter. But doing intervals—short bursts of fast-paced running with brief periods of walking or slow jogging in between—can jump-start it. Here's a sample workout you can do on a quarter-mile track: Warm up by running easy for 10 to 15 minutes. Then run one lap at a fast pace. (Don't go all-out.) Jog half a lap to recover; then do another lap hard. Repeat the cycle until you've completed six to eight fast laps, then jog for five to ten minutes to cool down. If you can't get to a track, you can do the same workout on the road. After warming up, pick up your pace for 1 minute, 30 seconds to 1 minute, 45 seconds. Walk or jog for an equal amount of time, and repeat.

3. Be creative. Once you get comfortable with interval workouts, you can vary the distance of your intervals from a quarter mile up to a mile. Walk or jog half your interval distance to give yourself enough rest between spurts. (If you're doing intervals on the road, use time instead of distance, giving yourself rests equal to the time it took you to run the interval.)

4. Slow down. "Even if you feel good, it pays to save your best efforts for your interval workouts," says Shorter. Most of your runs should be done at a pace 1 minute to 1 minute, 30 seconds slower than your 10K race pace. To keep yourself from competing with your watch, either leave it at home or run a course you're unfamiliar with so that you can't keep track of your mile splits.

5. Get flats. If you're running a race that's 10K (6.2 miles) or less, flats—ultralight running shoes that weigh between six and eight ounces—can boost your leg turnover. "That can save you a minute or more in a 10K race," says Shorter. For longer races, or if you weigh in at more than 180 pounds, you'll need a shoe with a bit more cushioning, like a lightweight trainer.

6. Pace yourself. Most long-distance world record holders run the second half of their races slightly faster than the first half. Instead of sprinting at the start, go out at about what feels like 80 percent of your maximum and try to shave off a second or two per mile. "If you go all-out at the beginning of a race and try to hang on at the end, you'll never run your best," says Shorter.

7. Join a running club. Having a coach and people to run with are the quickest ways to improve your running. To find a club in your area, contact the American Running and Fitness Association at (301) 913-9517.

MARATHON TRAINING
Jeff Galloway
Former Olympic marathoner turned coach and author of
Galloway's Book on Running (Shelter Publications, 1984)

*The following 17-week training program has helped thousands of runners
complete their first marathon. It assumes you can already run 5 miles comfortably—if not, add several weeks to the program, reducing the length of
all the runs to a level you can handle and work your way up slowly.
Although it has a success rate of over 98 percent, this program is designed to
get you through your first 26.2-mile ordeal on your feet, not to produce
world-class times. Wait till your second or third marathon before you think
about racing the distance.*

Here's a brief rundown on how to use the program:

1. *While your Tuesday and Thursday runs can be done at any pace you
like, all your Sunday long runs should be done at a leisurely pace—at least
two minutes per mile slower than your normal average speed. Novices can take
a one-minute walk break every two to three minutes from the beginning (and
throughout) every run. More experienced runners should take a one-minute
walk break every mile from the beginning of each long run. The slower pace
and interspersed walks will provide you with the same endurance as running
continuously—with a dramatic reduction in your injury risk.*

2. On your cross-training (XT) days, gradually build up to 45–60 minutes of nonpounding exercise that'll give your running muscles a chance to recover, while allowing you to continue to build your endurance. (Cycling, walking, swimming, water running and x-c skiing are best. Avoid stair climbing exercises, lower-body weight workouts and high-impact aerobics, like step.)

3. During the actual marathon use the same conservative pacing as you did in training. If you get past the halfway point feeling good, you can pick up the tempo gradually as you near the finish. Also, use walk breaks after every mile, starting at mile one.

JEFF GALLOWAY'S MARATHON PROGRAM

WEEK	MON	TUES	WED	THU	FRI	SAT	SUN
1	30 MIN WALK	30 MIN	XT	30 MIN	XT	OFF	7–8 MILES
2	30 MIN WALK	30 MIN	XT	30 MIN	XT	OFF	5 MILES
3	30 MIN WALK	30 MIN	XT	30 MIN	XT	OFF	9–10 MILES
4	30 MIN WALK	30 MIN	XT	30 MIN	XT	OFF	6 MILES
5	30 MIN WALK	30 MIN	XT	30 MIN	XT	OFF	12–13 MILES
6	30 MIN WALK	30 MIN	XT	30 MIN	XT	OFF	7 MILES
7	30 MIN WALK	30 MIN	XT	30 MIN	XT	OFF	15–16 MILES
8	30 MIN WALK	30 MIN	XT	30 MIN	XT	OFF	8–10 MILES

WEEK	MON	TUES	WED	THU	FRI	SAT	SUN
9	30 MIN WALK	30 MIN	XT	30 MIN	XT	OFF	18–19 MILES
10	30 MIN WALK	30 MIN	XT	30 MIN	XT	OFF	8–10 MILES
11	30 MIN WALK	30 MIN	XT	30 MIN	XT	OFF	20–22 MILES
12	30 MIN WALK	30 MIN	XT	30 MIN	XT	OFF	8–10 MILES
13	30 MIN WALK	30 MIN	XT	30 MIN	XT	OFF	8–10 MILES
14	30 MIN WALK	30 MIN	XT	30 MIN	XT	OFF	23–25 MILES
15	30 MIN WALK	30 MIN	XT	30 MIN	XT	OFF	8–10 MILES
16	30 MIN WALK	30 MIN	XT	30 MIN	XT	OFF	8–10 MILES
17	30 MIN WALK	30 MIN	XT	30 MIN	XT	OFF	MARATHON

Cycling

Chris Carmichael
National coaching director, United States Cycling Federation;
former member, U.S. Olympic cycling team; and former
professional cyclist who rode the Tour de France for
the 7-Eleven team

1. Give yourself a break. One week each month, cut your mileage and intensity by almost half. "Your body can't cope with week after week of hard training," says Carmichael. "By cutting back at regular intervals you can get more out of your workouts and you'll get stronger faster."

2. Spin the pedals. Pushing a high gear may seem to make you go faster over short distances, but studies have shown that cycling in lower gears at higher rpms actually produces more power. "Shoot for a cadence of 85 to 95 rpms," says Carmichael. "Anything slower and it'll look and feel like you're riding in oatmeal."

3. Sit in. On short, steep hills it's better to stand up and power your way up quickly. But on long climbs and gradual upgrades, it's much more efficient to shift down a gear or two and stay seated. "For anything over a quarter mile, stay in the saddle," says Carmichael.

4. Don't ride in running shoes. The soft cushioning that makes a running shoe worth its salt is exactly what makes it a bad cycling shoe. "Every time the sole flexes on the pedal, you lose power," says Carmichael. Stiff-soled cycling shoes with toe straps or clip-less pedals can easily boost your speed one to two miles per hour. In a pinch, use cross-training or court shoes. They're stiffer—and slightly faster—than running shoes.

5. Get new wheels. The lighter your bike, the faster you go—and the best way to lighten up is to buy a set of light, high-performance wheels with high-pressure tires, says Carmichael. "The wheels are constantly accelerating and decelerating, so taking the weight off there is most effective."

6. Go aero. At speeds over 25 miles an hour, wind resistance is your biggest enemy. If you have normal handlebars, get streamlined by sliding back on the saddle and bending at the waist—making your back as flat as possible—until you can almost kiss your handlebars. For triathletes and time trialists who do a lot of solo riding, clip-on aero bars are indispensable. One caveat: "Don't expect to race well with them right away," says Carmichael. "You'll have to move your seat forward a bit and get your muscles accustomed to the new position before you see your times drop."

7. Go on a big ride. When you're trying to build up your endurance for a long ride like a century, it's best to add 10 percent to your long ride every week and keep your other rides pretty much the same. Going long every time you're out will kill your training and motivation. (See sidebar titled Century Training.)

8. Get fit. "A bike that doesn't fit you is the biggest limiting factor in your ability to ride fast," says

Carmichael. While many bike shops have kits that can help you get a decent fit, working with a cycling coach or knowledgeable bike mechanic is the best way to fine-tune your positioning. If you want to do a rough assessment at home, have a friend hold the bike upright while you sit on the saddle. The right pedal should point down in almost a 5 o'clock position, as far away from your body as possible. With your cycling shoes on, straighten your right leg fully. If your bike fits properly, your heel will barely scrape the pedal or fall no more than half a centimeter above it. Anything higher or lower and you probably need to adjust your seat height.

CENTURY TRAINING
Dean Golich
Physiologist for the U.S. Cycling Team

*For most people, riding 100 miles on anything that doesn't have an engine
may seem a daunting—if not impossible—task. But with a few months of
dedication and the right training program, you can earn the right to
call yourself a "centurion."*

*The first training schedule is designed to make sure you get through your
first 100-mile ride unscathed. It assumes that
you're currently riding 50 to 70 miles a week.*

*The second training schedule is a bit more rigorous and is designed for cy-
clists who have already completed a century and are
looking to improve their performance.*

*Both programs dictate the mileage and speed of each training ride. Easy rides
are meant to be ridden at a comfortable pace throughout. Tempo rides are
more aggressive and should be ridden at the fastest pace you can maintain for
the entire ride without torturing yourself. Remember, when it comes to building killer endurance, the steadier the better.*

CENTURY TRAINING (SCHEDULE #1)

TRAINING TO COMPLETE A CENTURY

Week	Monday	Tuesday	Wednesday	Thursday	Friday	Saturday	Sunday
Pace		Easy	Tempo	Tempo	Easy	Easy	Tempo
1	off	10	15	20	10	25	25
2	off	15	20	25	10	30	30
3	off	15	20	25	15	35	35
4	off	10	15	20	15	40	35
5	off	15	20	25	15	30	30
6	off	20	25	30	off	35	30
7	off	25	30	35	off	40	35
8	off	15	20	25	20	30	30
9	off	20	25	30	off	45	40
10	off	25	30	35	off	50	45
11	off	30	35	40	off	50	50
12	off	20	25	30	10	45	30
13	off	30	35	40	off	55	60
14	off	20	20	30	10	10	Century

Tempo is the highest effort that can be sustained for the entire distance.
Easy is related to the how the workout is perceived, that is,
riding at a very comfortable pace.

CENTURY TRAINING (SCHEDULE #2)

TRAINING TO COMPLETE A CENTURY WITH BEST TIME

Week	Monday	Tuesday	Wednesday	Thursday	Friday	Saturday	Sunday
Pace		Easy	Tempo	Tempo	Easy	Easy	Tempo
1	off	10	15	20	10	25	25
2	off	15	20	25	10	30	30
3	off	15	20	25	15	35	35
4	off	10	15	20	15	40	35
5	off	15	30	25	15	30	30
6	off	20	25	30	off	35	30
7	off	25	30	35	off	60	35
8	off	15	30	25	off	40	40
9	off	20	35	30	off	75	40
10	off	25	30	35	off	50	45
11	off	30	35	40	off	70	50
12	off	20	40	30	off	80	30
13	off	30	35	40	off	55	60
14	off	20	20	30	off	10	Century

Tempo is the highest effort that can be sustained for the entire distance.
Easy is related to the how the workout is perceived, that is,
riding at a very comfortable pace.

Fly Fishing

Lefty Kreh
Fly fishing editor, *Fishing World* magazine; editor-at-large, *Fly Fisherman* magazine; author of several books, including *Lefty's Little Library* (available from Odysseus Editions, 2900 Cahaba Rd., Suite 101, Birmingham, AL 35223)

1. Take a casting lesson. If you can't cast 40 feet easily and accurately, you'll be a mediocre fly fisherman—at best. "If you can't shoot, you can't hunt, and if you can't cast, you can't fly fish," says Kreh. The sooner you take a lesson, the fewer bad habits you'll have to correct.

2. Don't ask your buddy for help. Many self-styled fly fishermen use improper technique, so even their best-intentioned advice is likely to hurt more than help.

3. Look at the scenery. The most important thing to do when fishing with dry flies is to look at the type of insects on the surface of the water and select a fly that's roughly the same shape, size and color. If your fly selection is limited, make sure you at least have a variety of shapes. "The shape is the most important factor," says Kreh. If you don't see any insects on the surface, use a wet fly.

4. Walk softly. "Water transmits sound about four-and-a-half times faster than air," says Kreh. "So don't wade into small streams if you don't have to." When you do walk out in the water, take it very slowly. "If you're making ripple marks more than two feet in front of you, you're going too fast. If they're 8 to 10 feet in front of you, pack it up—you've just told every fish in the area that you're in their pool."

5. Don't be a drag. It's very important to make your fly look as natural as possible, says Kreh. That means minimizing the drag your line puts on the fly. Make the tippett—the smallest, thinnest part of the leader that's tied to the fly—long and thin enough so that you see little squiggles in your leader when it's in the water. That builds some slack in the line so that the fly won't jerk every time you move your rod.

6. Obey the food chain. When using a wet fly like a crawfish or scalpin to catch trout, remember which is the predator and which is the bait. "A crawfish or scalpin would never swim up right in front of a trout," says Kreh. "Throw it a little behind and to one side of the fish to make it look like it's trying to sneak by."

7. Dry your flies to the side. When dry flies get soaked they tend to drown instead of sit on top of the water. Shake the fly out while it's on the line, but never do it over the area you're fishing. Spraying water over the fish tells them something's fishy.

8. Cast a shadow. When fishing at night or in muddy water, black, wet flies work best since they create a pronounced silhouette.

9. Be sharp. "A fish's mouth is rubber-tire tough," says Kreh. So using dull hooks will significantly reduce the number of fish you'll bring in. To check whether a hook is sharp enough, simply grab it by the eye and drag the point lightly across your thumbnail. If it digs in immediately, it's okay. If it slides even the slightest bit, you need to sharpen it.

10. Fish early and late. Trout get physiologically stressed and won't eat when the water temperature gets over 60. So if you're fishing in the summer, it's best to go out in the morning or at night.

11. I'll have a side of flies . . . and do you deliver? Fish would rather have their food brought to them than go get it themselves. Look for them to congregate around fast-moving sections of water where they sit and wait for food to go by. "Float your fly where you see the foam," says Kreh.

12. The calmer the water, the lighter the line. Anything you can do to reduce the impact you place on the water will improve your fishing, says Kreh. For relatively calm waters, go with a three- to four-weight line. Even in rougher waters, consider six-weight line the upper limit.

Basketball

Dick Vitale
ESPN college basketball analyst and author of four books on basketball, including his latest, *Dickie V's Top 40 All-Everything Teams* (Masters Press, 1994)

1. Create good shots. The reason great coaches like Coach K., Dean Smith and Lute Olson are consistent winners despite the fluctuations in their teams' talent is that they know how to set up good shots. "Keeping the ball and your body moving is the key," says Vitale. Know your range and work hard to get open within it.

2. Don't be a Kodak moment. If you stand around and watch one of your teammates drive to the hoop, you've immediately given the other team a man advantage. When you don't have the ball,

you should be cutting to the basket ready to receive a pass or cutting away from the ball to set a screen for another player.

3. Step off the screen. After setting a screen, take a step back and look for a pass. "Defenses often double-team on the guy who is working off the pick," says Vitale. That means you'll probably be open for an easy jumper.

4. Face the basket. After you catch a pass, always turn to face the basket. "That puts you in what I call 'triple-threat formation,' " says Vitale. If your man is playing off you, you'll have an open shot. If he comes up, you can drive around him to the basket or pass to one of your teammates cutting through the lane.

5. "Ya gotta play D, baby." If you're playing good defense, you shut down *their* shot selection. "It's reverse psychology," says Vitale. And when you're on the playground you have to go man. Making a zone defense work well takes team practice, says Vitale.

6. Get in shape. The more you can move without getting tired, the better your game. At least once a week, skip your lunch-hour game and dedicate the time to doing sprints, suicides and lateral movement drills.

7. When you're playing half-court, pass. The key to winning in half-court games is to reverse the ball back and forth across the court quickly until you break the defense and get the open shot.

8. When you're playing full-court, run. Working fast transitions is the easiest way to win. "Create breaks, run the lanes and look to get easy shots off a 3-on-2 or 4-on-2," says Vitale. If the defense consistently gets back before you, move the ball as you would in a half-court game.

9. Don't palm the ball. To make a good shot, square your body to the basket, aim for just over the front of the rim and shoot the ball off your fingertips—not your palm. Done properly, the ball will have a smooth backspin on it.

10. Forget about playing horse. Shooting around haphazardly doesn't do much to build the concentration you need, says Vitale. Instead, do what the pros do: Select a spot on the floor about three to four feet away from the basket and shoot from that spot until you make three in a row. Then move to another spot and stay there until you make another three in a row. Repeat until you reach the outer limit of your range.

Getting Good Playoff Seats

John Langbein
President, Ticket Exchange, Phoenix, Arizona

1. Have a plan. "Don't count on the price or name of the seat to tell you how good it is," says Langbein. " 'Upper box' can often mean nosebleed." To do business with a scalper or a ticket broker, you need a diagram of the stadium showing where all the seats are. Since most box offices run out of schematics late in the season, buy a program outside the stadium or check the front of the local phone book. (Most cities with a professional sports team include schematics there.) To get a head start on next season, put in a request for a season ticket application and the stadium will mail you a seating chart.

2. Make sure you've got the right game. Since playoff tickets are printed well before the series begins, they usually don't include the date of the game. Look at the abbreviation in the "Date" section of the ticket. Most often you'll find a letter followed by a number—like A1 or B4. The letter stands for the playoff round, while the number represents the game. For example, a ticket labeled B4 would be for the fourth game of the second round.

3. Be patient. For most games, you can save yourself a lot of money by waiting until just after the game begins before buying a ticket from a scalper. "But it doesn't always work that way," says Langbein. "For really big games, you may wind up listening to it on the radio if you wait too long."

4. "Sold out" doesn't mean sold out. "Regardless of what they say, all ticket offices hold a couple hundred seats for emergencies or oversights," says Langbein. These tickets are normally released through the main stadium box office without notice on game day. "The only way you'll find out about these tickets is to go hang out in front of the box office three or four hours before the game."

5. Shop around and bargain. Unless someone is willing to sell you good seats at or near face value, don't buy the first tickets you see. "To get the best deal from a scalper or broker you have to know the market," says Langbein. "Shop around with half a dozen other sellers before you buy." Once you find a reasonable offer, ask the seller to knock 10 to 15 percent off his price. "It almost always works if you don't give in, but if the guy's willing to let you get away for a measly 10 percent, you know you got his best deal," says Langbein.

6. Use a broker for business. Although scalpers are legal in about half the states, that doesn't mean you won't get in trouble if you buy from one. "Scalpers sometimes steal tickets out of mailboxes or make counterfeit ones, so when you go to take your seats the holders of the legitimate tickets can have security haul you out," says Langbein. You won't get arrested, but it doesn't look good in front of a client or the boss. When buying tickets to a "sold-out" game for business, it's best to use a ticket broker. Most brokers keep lists of season ticket holders and pay them enough to watch the game at home. "But brokers can be shady too," adds Langbein. Before shelling out any money, call your local Better Business Bureau and ask if any complaints have been filed against the broker you're dealing with. One or two grievances, and the broker's probably OK. But if there's more than five, shop elsewhere.

Triathlon

Dave Scott
Six-time Hawaiian Ironman champion and coach of Dave Scott's
Triathlon Training Camps in Boulder, CO

1. Focus on your cycling. "Since 60 percent of the average triathlon is spent on the bike, the fastest way to improve your overall performance is to improve your cycling," says Scott.

2. Work on your technique. One of the biggest mistakes novices make is to overemphasize conditioning and neglect technique. "If you don't have good technique, your rate of improvement is going to be minimal, no matter how hard you train," says Scott. Spend at least one workout a week per sport concentrating on your form.

3. Get taped. It's nearly impossible to detect minor problems in your form just by feel. Have a friend shoot a videotape of you doing all three sports. That will make it easier for you to see what you're doing wrong and to make the necessary adjustments.

4. Build a strong midsection. The majority of your power in any sport comes from your abs, hips, hamstrings and lower back, says Scott. Keeping those areas strong and flexible can boost your speed and prevent injuries.

5. Don't race yourself into shape. At the beginning of every season, give yourself six weeks of base training before your first race. "If you absolutely have to do a particular race before the six weeks are up, do one leg hard and cruise through the rest," says Scott.

6. Take it easy. "If half your workouts are hard, you're doing too much and slowing your progress," says Scott. "Only about one in every five workouts should really make you work."

7. Get aero bars. Wind tunnel tests have shown that putting a pair of aerodynamic handlebars on your bike can save you up to two minutes over a 25-mile course. One caveat: To get the most out of the bars, you'll have to move your seat forward a bit and spend a few weeks getting your muscles accustomed to the new position.

8. Treat transitions as a fourth sport. Since the clock never stops in triathlons, slow changes between events can be a huge waste of time. "Why bust your butt training to run ten seconds faster per mile if you're just going to waste it sitting down to put on your shoes?" says Scott. Timing your swim-bike and bike-run transitions during practice will save you time in a race.

9. Know the transition area. In the heat of a race, it can seem like a maze. "Knowing which way to enter and exit on each leg *before* the race can keep you from losing valuable time," says Scott.

10. Drink up. Even slight dehydration can be a serious drain on your performance. For two days before a race, keep a water bottle by your side and sip from it constantly. "If your urine isn't clear and you don't get up at least once the night before the race to go to the bathroom, you're not drinking enough," says Scott.

11. Eat something. Even the most conditioned athletes have only about a two-hour supply of carbohydrates tucked away in their muscles and liver. So if your race will last longer than that, take in at least a few hundred calories per additional hour to avoid "the wall." If you can't stand to eat solid food during the race, try a sports drink or some watered-down juice.

12. Don't do more than two races a month. "If you race every weekend, you'll waste most of your weekly training time recovering from one race and resting for the next," says Scott.

Volleyball

Steve Timmons
Three-time U.S. Olympic medalist in volleyball; member, 1986 World Indoor Champion team; gold medalist, 1987 Pan Am Games; currently ranked in the top ten on the Pro Beach Volleyball Tour

1. Take your eye off the ball. "If you only watch the ball, it'll be by you before you have time to react," says Timmons. Instead, watch the hitter's shoulders and angle of approach, and position yourself accordingly.

2. Wait on the ball. If you rush to position yourself underneath a set, you'll lose your momentum for the hit. "Wait for a second—then attack the ball by jumping into it," says Timmons.

3. It's not in the wrist. When you're passing the ball, it should hit off your forearms, not your wrists. The reason? Your forearms are more forgiving and less likely to send the ball careening off to the side.

4. Use two arms when you bump. "Even experienced players are about 80 percent more accurate when they use two arms instead of one," says Timmons.

5. Practice your jump. The best way to improve your vertical leap is to do plyometrics—power-producing jumping drills. A basic drill goes like this: Place a piece of tape on a wall, eight feet above the floor. Then, standing one foot away from the wall, jump with your arms above your head as if you were going up for a block. (If you're a hitter, jump with one arm extended.) Once you land, *immediately* go back up for another jump. Start with three sets of five jumps, spending as little time as possible on the floor between jumps. You can increase your sets to ten jumps after one month. A safety note: Plyometrics can give your knees a beating. Do them only two or three times a week on days you don't have a match or lift with your legs.

6. Drop a few pounds. Not only will it help you jump higher, it'll also keep you from getting tired during the late stages of a long match and putting your knees to an early death.

7. Don't wear basketball shoes. They're often too heavy for volleyball, because basketball players need much more support. "Volleyball shoes have the right mix of lightness and cushioning to maximize your performance," says Timmons. And their reinforced toes provide protection when you dive.

8. Get into position. "The most important thing you can do to improve your reaction time is to be in position to hit the ball *before* it gets to you," says Timmons. That means knees bent, back straight and arms out in front. If you have to reach for the ball, you'll have less control.

9. On the beach, go for control—not the kill. "Indoors, you usually have to slam the ball to win a point," says Timmons. "But beach volleyball is much less of a power game. If you get into trouble, just hit to the corners and the ball will usually go down."

Tennis

Vic Braden
Teaching pro for 40 years, founder and president of the Vic Braden Tennis College, and adviser, *Tennis* magazine

1. Start with lessons. "Once you've been playing a while, it's hard to reprogram your strokes," says Braden. So if you're thinking of taking up the game, don't rely on a buddy to teach you. "Take five or six lessons with a good teaching pro and you'll develop the right strokes for life."

2. Don't use the ball machine. "Your brain's retrieval system doesn't have to work very hard when you're hitting the same shot over and over," says Braden. To win on the court, you have to become accustomed to working at a much higher level of concentration.

3. Hit one more shot. "Even at the pro level, players don't win games as often as their opponents lose them," says Braden. "The more opportunities you give your opponent to make a mistake, the better you'll do." Instead of trying to put the ball away as soon as you can, just keep it in play. "If you hit one more ball than usual on every rally, you'll beat more than half the players who now beat you."

4. Go crosscourt instead of down the line. "Taking a ball down the line when it's coming at you on an angle is the most difficult shot in tennis," says Braden. Add that to the fact that tennis courts are almost five feet longer diagonally than they are from baseline to baseline, and it's easy to see why hitting crosscourt greatly improves your chances of keeping the ball in play.

5. Keep your head down. While you can never actually see the ball hit your racket (because it happens too fast for your brain to record), it's a good idea to keep your head down until after you've finished your follow-through. "Even though your brain has the shot figured out before the ball gets to your racket, studies have shown that lifting your head before you hit a shot changes the ball's flight pattern," says Braden.

6. Know when to attack. In general, the best time to come to the net is after you've hit the ball deep to your opponent's backhand.

7. Take your racket for a test drive. While oversize rackets have a larger sweet spot and can give you more power than conventional rackets, it is possible to get one that's too big. "Never buy a racket without playing with it first," says Braden. "If it doesn't feel right on your first few hits, it's not the right racket for you."

8. Lift right. Curls and bench presses won't do much for your tennis game. So when you're in the gym focus on the muscles that matter—your legs, abs, back and shoulders. Pay special attention to your upper back, rear deltoids and rotator cuffs—they're the most neglected muscles in tennis. If they are not strong, you're going to get injured.

9. Be fluid. "A powerful serve comes from smoothly transferring force from your legs to your upper body," says Braden. "If you tense up and try to muscle the ball, you'll break the flow and lose power."

10. Don't throw the ball straight up. For a stronger serve, toss the ball out in front of you and explode into it.

Swimming

Rowdy Gaines
Winner of three gold medals in the 1984 Olympics and coach of
the Oahu Masters' Swim Team

1. Hone your skills. For most swimmers, technique—not conditioning—is the biggest factor limiting their swimming speed. If you're taking more than 25 strokes per 25 meters (23 strokes per 25 yards), you need to spend at least half of your training time improving your technique. To get help, ask a local swim coach to take a look at your stroke, or contact the U.S. Master's Swimming Association at (508) 886-6631 for the number of your local swim team.

2. Get streamlined on your push-off. When pushing off the wall, place one hand on top of the other, wrap your top thumb around the hand underneath and press your biceps against the back of your ears as you glide through the water. "If your push-off isn't getting you to the flags—which are five meters from the wall—you need to work on your positioning," says Gaines.

3. Go deep. When pushing off the wall, go under the water one or two feet. That way, you'll avoid the turbulence you created on the way in.

4. Make the first stroke powerful. Since it preserves the momentum of your push-off, the first stroke after your glide is the most important one on each length. "There's no way you can swim as fast as you're going when you push off the wall," says Gaines. "But the better your first stroke, the less you'll slow down."

5. Move your hips. A good part of a swimmer's power comes from the hips. To get the most out of every stroke, roll your hips and shoulders into the water.

6. Be consistent. Since swimming involves technique *and* endurance, you need to swim at least three times a week to stay up on your game. "Five days one week and one day the next won't cut it," says Gaines.

7. Mix it up. If you do the same workout every time you swim you'll see little, if any, progress. By alternating among different types of swim training, like sprints, kicks, pulls, drills and fartleks (continuous swims that alternate between fast and slow spurts), you can develop all aspects of your conditioning and improve much more quickly. Most swim teams offer a wide variety of workouts for beginners and advanced swimmers. But if practice doesn't fit into your schedule, just ask the coach for a few sample workouts to do on your own.

8. Don't do curls. Weight lifting can improve your swimming if you do the right exercises. "Focus on your legs, lats, chest and abs," says Gaines. "The rest of the stuff is mainly for show."

9. Split your season. To get the most out of your weight lifting, work hard to improve your strength during the off-season, when you're not competing. Then, as the season rolls around, cut your lifting in half and do just enough to maintain your strength. If you lift hard and swim hard during the same season, your muscles won't get enough rest and neither your strength, nor your swimming, will improve very much.

10. Get loose. Flexible ankles are the mark of a good freestyle swimmer. To test your ankle flexibility, sit on the floor with your legs extended straight in front of you. Point your toes forward and try to make them touch the floor. World-class freestylers can lay their feet flat, but if you can get within an inch or two of the floor, you're in good shape. If not, have a friend press down gently on the tops of your feet for 30 seconds, three times a day, three or four days a week.

Racquetball

Cliff Swain
Four-time professional racquetball world champion

1. Control center court. After every shot, make an attempt to get back to the middle of the court. From there, you can hit the ball harder, cover more angles and screen the guy behind you.

2. Hit low. It's simple physics—the lower you hit the ball off the front wall, the less time your opponent has to get it.

3. Don't spin the ball. Unlike tennis players, who can use spin to their advantage, racquetball players should hit the ball as flat as possible. If you put spin on a racquetball, it slows the ball down and can also make it pop up after it hits the wall, giving your opponent an easy target. "You want the ball to go straight in and come straight out," says Swain.

4. Serve to your opponent's backhand. "Even for the best players, the backhand is naturally the weaker shot," says Swain.

5. Use a change-up. "Plastering the ball isn't always the best strategy," says Swain. Including some slower shots in the mix will throw off your opponent's timing and give you the edge.

6. Bigger isn't always better. While an oversized racquet can give you a definite advantage, buying the biggest one you can find isn't a good idea. "Monster-size racquets will slow your swing and make you lose the feel of the ball," says Swain. Choose a graphite racquet with a 102-square-inch head.

7. Glove down. When buying a glove for your racquet hand, it's best to get one size smaller than you'd normally wear. "The torque and sweat of the game will make the glove—and racquet—slip in your hand if it isn't real tight," says Swain.

8. Move your feet. "To get the most power on a shot you have to move to the ball and have your feet under you," says Swain. "If you lunge or reach for it, you won't get any power."

9. Go with mid-cut shoes. High-tops don't give you the ankle mobility to make very sharp cuts, while low-cut models don't supply enough support. Proper fit is also essential. "If your feet slide inside the shoes, it will take you longer to recover between shots," says Swain. "If you're between sizes, go down a half size."

10. Make your opponent run on each shot. A tired enemy is the best kind.

11. Practice as you play. In games, you're most likely to have to hit shots on the run. So during warm-ups or practice, keep moving.

Mountain Biking

Ned Overend
Six-time U.S. champion and 1990 World Cross Country champion

1. Learn how to use your brakes. "Brakes are the easiest way to maintain control, but they can be also the easiest way to *lose* it," says Overend. "Locking up the brakes—especially the front one—compromises your ability to steer and roll over stuff." Instead, slow down gradually *before* you get to rocky stretches or hard turns and release the front brake as you steer through the area.

2. Slide back before throwing out the anchor. "The more weight you have *behind* your braking wheel, the faster you'll be able to stop and the less chance you'll have of doing a face plant over the bars," says Overend. "If you have to jam on the brakes, slide your butt back as far as it will go before you do it."

3. On hills, positioning is everything. On steep downhills, keeping your butt way back on the seat will keep you from being thrown over your handlebars. "On uphills, it's more of a balancing act," says Overend. "You want your weight on the back for traction, but you also want some weight on the front wheel to keep it on the ground and allow you to steer." To get in the best climbing position, stay in the saddle, bend at the waist and lean over your handlebars. As the terrain begins to level out, you can sit up some because there's less chance you'll pull your front wheel off the ground.

4. Stand up right. If a climb is too steep to make sitting in the saddle, stand up with your butt over the saddle and your body bent forward at the waist. "If you stand straight up, you'll lose all your traction in the back," says Overend.

5. Get a shock for the long haul. By helping to keep your front wheel on the ground, front shock absorbers give you more steering power over bumpy trails. Also, shocks can help you save energy on long rides by sucking up most of the jarring bumps that would otherwise have to be absorbed by your arm and shoulder muscles.

6. Learn how to do a wheelie. The ability to pick your front end off the ground at least a few inches can help you clear most of the common obstacles you'll encounter. To do it right, slide your butt back to take the weight off the front end, give the pedal a forceful downward stroke and pull up *gently* on the handlebars. (For small logs and low curbs, just remove the weight from the front end and let the bike roll over the obstacle.) Once your front wheel is on top of the obstacle, stand up to lighten the back end, and pull it over.

7. Go with clip-in pedals. Pedals like Shimano SPDs that connect to your shoes like a ski binding connects to a boot give you considerably more power and control than standard pedals or toe clips, says Overend. They also make it easier to restart if your foot pops off the pedal on a steep uphill or downhill.

8. Get bar ends. Bullhornlike handlebar extenders help you get the extra leverage you need to stomp down on the pedals during steep climbs. "The higher a grip you can get, the more power you'll have," says Overend. Bar ends also give you more positions for your hands, reducing the chance your fingers will go numb on a long ride.

9. Ease up when downshifting. To keep your chain from jamming up between your chainrings and frame when you shift from the middle chainring to the small one, take a little pressure off the pedals as you shift down. "Always downshift before you get to a hill," says Overend. "That way you won't have to downshift as you stomp on the pedals."

10. Control inflation. Most novices don't put enough air in their tires and as a result wind up with lots of flats. On the flip side, using too much air will cause you to bounce all over the trail. "Thirty to 40 pounds of pressure in your knobbies provides flat protection *and* gives you maximum traction and control," says Overend. If you're doing most of your riding on the road, bald tires with 60 to 70 pounds of pressure will provide plenty of traction and reduce your rolling resistance, enabling you to go faster.

Golf

Nick Price
1993 and 1994 PGA Player of the Year

1. Underestimate yourself. Amateurs often make the mistake of choosing a club based on their best performance with it. "If you're 175 yards away from the pin and your longest shot with your five iron was 175 yards, you'd probably be better off hitting a four," says Price. "Hitting one club longer than you think you need on each shot can significantly reduce your score, especially when you consider that most trouble is usually in front of the green."

2. Don't overcompensate. Many players who have a slice or a hook try to correct it by pointing their feet or aiming their shots in the opposite direction, says Price. But in reality, this "quick fix" usually exaggerates the problem. "The frustrating thing about golf is that common sense doesn't always work," he says. Until a golf pro shows you exactly what you're doing wrong, it's best to live with your hook or slice. Otherwise, you run the risk of screwing up what's *right* about your swing.

3. Work on your short game. Nearly two-thirds of all the shots in golf occur within 100 yards of the hole. "To get the most out of your practice time, skip the driving range and work on your chipping and putting," says Price.

4. Practice under pressure. That will help you build up the nerves of steel you'll need to sink a 12-footer to win the office tournament, according to scientific studies. To create a pressure situation during practice, go out to the green and imagine that your boss or wife is watching your shot and heckling you. Once you get yourself worked up, take a deep breath, go through your normal preshot routine and take the shot without contemplating the consequences.

5. Get the proper fit. Your height's not all you need to consider when buying the right club. "I'm six feet tall, but I have long arms, so I have to use shorter clubs than the average six-footer," says Price. The bottom line: Have a golf pro measure you and inspect your swing before you buy your clubs. "Using the wrong equipment changes your posture and can easily add ten strokes to your game, or leave you injured," says Price.

6. Stay loose. Muscling the ball off the tee produces more sore backs than awe-inspiring drives. To get the most distance, keep a loose grip on the club and concentrate on getting a smooth windup and follow-through. "Power comes from club speed, not bulging muscles," says Price.

7. Get a washboard. The best muscles to build for golf are your abdominals, not your biceps. A strong midsection will not only help you produce a more forceful follow-through, but it's also the easiest way to shore up your back against injury.

8. Let technology help you. If they're not already in your bag, adding metal woods and perimeter-weighted irons can make a big difference. Both clubs have a larger sweet spot than their traditional counterparts, which can put a mis-hit in the first cut of the rough instead of in the woods.

GAMES

Nintendo

Mike Iarossi
1994 Nintendo PowerFest Champion

1. Choose the best weapon. "Without the right controller, you're at a huge disadvantage," says Iarossi. For fighting games like Mortal Kombat and Street Fighter II, large, arcade-type joysticks give you the best control. For shoot-'em-up games, or anything that requires a heavy trigger finger, turbo controllers are standard issue. And for driving games, the traditional joypad makes it easier to go to the right and left without oversteering.

2. Patience is a virtue—sometimes. In fighting games, the more time you spend observing your opponents' patterns and planning a targeted response, the better you'll do. "If you jump right in throwing every punch and kick you've got, you're gonna get smeared," says Iarossi.

3. And sometimes it isn't. When it comes to sports games—whether you're playing your computer or your buddy—getting an early lead is crucial for controlling the tempo of the game. "Do whatever it takes to get on top quick—throw the bomb, run the blitz—anything," says Iarossi. "If you get burned on a big play, come back with something even bigger."

4. Get an education. You'll always benefit by reading the instructions. However, if you read them before you've started playing, chances are you won't pick up many of the subtleties. The best plan? Read the instructions several times. Once before you start, once after you've been playing for an hour or two, and any time you get stuck. And if you're playing a strategy game loaded with options (say, SimCity), consider studying—not just reading—the instructions.

5. Don't take advice from just anybody. When it comes to gaming tips, not all sources are created equal. *Die-Hard Game Fan* (Die-Hard Publications) and *Electronic Gaming Monthly* (Sendai Publications) provide the best inside info around.

6. Be a bully. In adventure games, spending a little extra time early on fighting easy foes will help you build up experience points that can save your skin down the road. "At any time during the game, the computer expects you to be at a certain level," says Iarossi. "If you're just a little bit above that, you'll have an easier go of it."

7. Check your arsenal. "If an area seems impossible to get through, you probably don't have the right equipment," says Iarossi. "Go back and look for objects or areas you might have missed that'll help you beef up."

8. Be organized. In strategy games, it's essential to develop a plan early on and stick with it. "For example, to be successful in SimCity, you have to build neatly right from the start," says Iarossi.

Eating Contests

Frank Pastore

Ex–major league baseball player and record holder for the steak-eating contest at the Big Texan Steak Ranch in Amarillo, Texas. Consumed a shrimp cocktail, dinner salad, buttered roll, baked potato and 72-ounce steak in nine and a half minutes.

1. Don't chew. In eating contests, chewing is the biggest waste of time. So, as you go, cut the food into bite-size pieces. "Then chomp down once and swallow," says Pastore.

2. Sharpen your tools. "A dull knife can slow you down significantly," says Pastore. "To maximize your speed you have to be cutting faster than you're swallowing."

3. Use both hands. Once you have all your food cut, you can use the tip of your knife—as well as your fork—to shovel food into your mouth.

4. Stay off the sweets. Although they may taste good, sugary foods will make you feel full faster than other eats. So, if you have the choice, skip the pie and the ice cream.

5. Keep the food moist. "The wetter the food, the easier it is to cut and the less saliva you need to get it down," says Pastore, who used a whole bottle of steak sauce during his record-setting performance. "I always order my steak rare or medium rare."

6. Stay hydrated. Not drinking during the contest for the sake of saving time will actually make it harder for you to get the food down in a hurry. Take small sips whenever you feel yourself getting dry.

7. Don't starve yourself. "Fasting the day or two before the contest shrinks your stomach, and you'll actually be able to eat less," says Pastore. Eat normally up to the day of the contest, then have light meals on the big day.

8. Get some exercise. Working out before the big meal can help boost your appetite, but don't do it right before you eat. Studies have shown that exercising too close to mealtime can actually curb your hunger by raising your body temperature. Swimming in a cold pool or working out a few hours before you eat is best.

9. Don't stop. "Taking a break allows the fullness to catch up with you," says Pastore. "Keep eating until you can't eat any more, then give up."

Shooting Pool

Allen Hopkins
Winner, 1993 Challenge of Champions; number-one-ranked player on pro billiards tour, 1990; two-time winner, U.S. Open (1977 and 1981); two-time world champion (1977 and 1985)

1. Stay down. "Popping your head and torso up before you finish your follow-through is the surest way to mishit," says Hopkins.

2. Don't stare at the cue ball. Once you line up your shot, focus your aim on the object ball at the spot where you want the cue ball to hit.

3. Lighten up. The biggest mistake amateurs make is that they hit the cue ball too hard. "The harder you hit it, the more likely you are to knock it off line," says Hopkins.

4. Be a straight shooter. If your accuracy isn't up to snuff, the problem may be that you're trying to do too much, too soon. "At first, it's very important to get comfortable making all your shots by hitting the center of the cue ball," says Hopkins. Once you get the basics down cold, *then* take a lesson to learn the proper way to apply English.

5. Don't use a cue stick with a flat tip. "Hitting a round ball with a round tip improves your accuracy," says Hopkins. "Also, without a round tip, you can't apply any English."

6. Chalk after every shot. A fresh layer of chalk on the cue tip will keep it from slipping when it hits the ball. For advanced players, the chalk also provides the friction necessary to generate English.

7. Get on-line. To figure out the angle on a tough shot, try this little trick: Say you're trying to sink the four ball into a side pocket. Take an extra ball and place it next to the four ball in line with the side pocket you're aiming for. Aim the cue ball at the center of the extra ball and just before you hit your shot, have a friend remove the extra ball. With a little practice, lining up these shots will become second nature.

8. Check your balance. The firmer your feet are planted on the floor *before* the shot, the less likely you'll be to screw up *during* the shot. Whenever possible, avoid shots that have you twisting yourself around the table like a contortionist.

Rotisserie League Baseball

Dan Okrent
Managing editor, *Life* magazine, and creator of Rotisserie League baseball

1. Look for players with consistency. "Hitting and speed are more predictable than pitching," says Okrent. If a guy hits for average or steals a lot of bases one year, you can assume he'll do the same next season. Pitchers, on the other hand, are more likely to be erratic.

2. Spend wisely. It's been statistically proven that it's better to spend more money on offense than on defense. Sink 60 to 63 percent of your loot into assembling a high-powered hitting force. Spend the balance on your pitching staff.

3. Watch who you turn to for advice. First-year players who haven't yet made a name for themselves can be great deals, if you make the right picks. Bill James—author of the annual *Stats Minor League Handbook* (Stats, Inc., 800-637-8287)—has the best record for predicting a player's major-league performance based on how he did in the minors, says Okrent. On the other hand, don't listen to what Sparky Anderson has to say about rookies. "If everything he said was right, guys would make it from AA ball to the Hall of Fame in two weeks."

4. Give up one category, but never two. "Seven times out of ten, you can come in last in one category and still take the pennant," says Okrent. But give up two, and you don't have a chance of making it to the middle of October.

5. Go on the road. Because all your buddies are likely to bid on the local heroes, they're usually overpriced. Avoid the home team whenever possible.

6. Bench Wade Boggs. "Players who hit .300 but lack power or speed are usually poor investments because they only produce in one category," says Okrent.

7. Look for young blood. Offensive players usually peak around age 27 or 28. So, for the most part, it's wiser to go with lesser-known 24- to 28-year-olds rather than big-name, overpriced, 32-year-olds.

8. Go for the heat. Fastball pitchers are more likely to hold their form than junk pitchers, who rely heavily on curves and change-ups, says Okrent.

9. Who's on first? What's on second? As in the majors, your team should have power hitters behind the plate and at the corners—both in the infield and outfield. Your center fielder and middle infielders should be fleet of foot.

10. Know the parks. For example, it pays to know that Oakland is a terrible hitter's park, while Wrigley Field will wreak havoc on pitchers. So stay away from hitters traded to the A's and pitchers traded to the Cubs.

11. Avoid closers who play for Buck Showalter, Jim Leyland and Tommy Lasorda. "All three of them believe in 'bullpen-by-committee,'" says Okrent. A relief pitcher who had 40 saves a year with one team and who gets traded to one of these guys will see his total go down to 20."

12. Develop your statistical power. Roti-Stats in California at (800) 676-7684 produces some of the most comprehensive and easiest-to-read stats around. The better your stats, the better your chances.

Beer Chugging

Steve Petrosino
World record holder for chugging a liter of beer—1.9 seconds

1. Open your throat. "Every time you swallow, you double your time," says Petrosino. "To drink a beer really fast, pull your tongue back, suppress the gag reflex, and pour it straight down." If you can't "open your throat," take large mouthfuls of beer and take as few swallows as possible.

2. Use a pilsner glass. When you turn a standard beer mug upside down, an air pocket forms at the bottom that holds the beer in the cylinder for a second. In a pilsner glass, which has a cone-shaped bottom, there's little room for an air pocket to form, so the beer comes out quicker. "It's a perfect chugging vessel," says Petrosino.

3. Shoot from the hip. "After doing computerized fluid analyses, we found that the only way I could break the world record was to accelerate the beer before it got to my mouth," says Petrosino. "So when I set the world record, I actually started with the glass at my hip and snapped it up so that the beer would already be flying by the time it hit my throat." But the hip launch isn't for everyone—especially if you already have a couple of beers in you. "It can cost you a couple hundred bucks in dental work," he says.

4. Split it up. If you're going for the liter record, it's best to break it up into two half-liters before you chug. "I tried

every possible combination, and that's what went down the fastest," says Petrosino. "Bigger glasses are unwieldy and switching between too many smaller glasses will slow you down."

5. The flatter, the better. "Highly carbonated beers expand in the back of your throat and can make it feel like you're trying to swallow a balloon," says Petrosino. In general, European beers (English ales like Bass Ale, in particular) have less carbonation—and are better for chugging—than most American brands.

6. Drink warm beer. "A warm liquid can't hold as much dissolved gas as a cold one," says Petrosino. So the warmer the beer, the flatter it'll be and the faster it will go down. Also, a cold beer can cause your throat to constrict, making it nearly impossible to drink in a hurry.

7. Stir it. Swirling your finger in the beer before you drink it helps remove some of the carbonation. "Every little bit helps," says Petrosino.

Monopoly

Gary Peters
First person inducted into the Monopoly Hall of Fame and winner
of the 1987 and 1991 national Monopoly tournaments

1. Buy everything. During your first three or four trips around the board, buy every property you land on. Then, once you have seven or eight, you can be more selective. "To win, you need to have a variety of properties you can trade with," says Peters.

2. Be wary of trading away monopolies. Unless you're getting one in return, never trade away a property that gives your opponent a monopoly. "Even if he offers you two or three times what you paid for it, don't do it," says Peters. If you have to sell to get yourself out of debt, wait until your piece passes the would-be monopoly. Otherwise, you might run smack into a chain of hotels built on some of your former land.

3. Develop quickly. Build three houses on a property as fast as possible—that practically doubles the rent you'd receive for two houses. It's especially crucial if your opponent is seven squares (the most common dice roll) away from one of your monopolies, says Peters. "In that case, do everything in your power—auction other properties, take out mortgages, *anything*—to get your three houses up."

4. **Wait on the hotels.** Razing three houses to put up a hotel gives you only a minor increase in rent, so it's better to put three houses on all your monopolies before you get into the hotel business.

5. **Buy the red and orange.** Computer analyses have shown that these properties are landed on the most, and so are the most valuable. "If you can afford to develop it, red's the biggest killer of them all," says Peters.

6. **Don't try to make a living off Boardwalk and Park Place.** While they bring in penthouse-sized rents, the blue properties aren't landed on enough to make them your bread and butter. "You'll win more games developing your red or orange properties first," says Peters.

7. **Buy the railroads—forget about the utilities.** "Railroads are the cash cow in Monopoly," says Peters. "If you can get all four, you'll have enough money to build anything you want."

Lottery

Sam Valenza
Publisher, *Lottery Player's* magazine

1. Don't play dates. Picking birthdays and anniversaries tends to limit you to low numbers. And since many people use this method, chances are you'll have to share your winnings. "Lottery numbers are picked randomly, so that's the way you should do it," says Valenza. "Let the computer pick for you or pick them out of a hat."

2. Play the wheel. The most intelligent way to play Lotto games is to pick numbers at random and then "wheel" them into all the possible combinations. Say you're playing a six-number Lotto game. Pick seven numbers out of a hat and play all the possible six-number combinations that can be created from those seven numbers. (Seven numbers can be wheeled into 8 six-number combinations, eight numbers can be wheeled into 26 combinations, nine into 56, 10 into 210, etc.) Playing a wheel system won't improve your odds of winning the big prize, but it will increase the number of prizes you win if you get four or five numbers right, says Valenza. To obtain a simple wheeling computer, contact *Lottery Player's* magazine at (800) 367-9681.

3. Don't splurge on instant lottery. Instant lottery games are set up so that there are a certain number of winners in each region. But that doesn't mean each store in a given area has the same number of big prizes, so buying a lot of tickets from one store doesn't assure you of winning big. "You'll have the same odds—and more fun—if you buy a few here and a few there," says Valenza.

Betting on the Horses

Andy Beyer
Horse racing columnist for *The Washington Post* who created the Beyer Speed Figure—one of the premier handicapping tools—for the *Daily Racing Form*. Author of four handicapping books, including his latest, *Beyer on Speed* (Houghton-Mifflin, 1993)

1. Bet on the fastest horse. It's not as simple as it sounds. Many odds-makers handicap horses by looking at those they've raced against and those they've beaten, not how fast they run. "Raw speed is more important," says Beyer. The Beyer Speed Figure (featured in the *Daily Racing Form*) assigns each horse a numerical performance rating that reflects only the horse's speed—the higher the number, the faster the horse. "Thirty percent of the time, the horse with the top speed figure in the race will win," he says. "That's not a bad head start."

2. Stay up on current events. "A horse's most recent race is the best indicator of the shape he's in," says Beyer. While the *Daily Racing Form* gives you speed figures for a horse's last ten races, focus primarily on the most recent figure.

3. Look at the trainer, not the jockey. "The trainer has more to do with a horse's success," says Beyer. "A horse that has a trainer with a high winning percentage always deserves respect." Be wary of a horse that has a trainer with a losing record, even if he looks good otherwise.

4. Don't be ultraconservative. Sure, betting a favorite to show is almost a sure way of winning, but it won't give you much of a return. "Over the long haul it pays to take more risks," says Beyer. "You'll cash fewer bets, but you'll win more money."

5. Go with the exacta. Exacta bets—in which you pick the first and second horse in order—are just about the best bets you can make. "You get great odds and pay-offs for logical choices," says Beyer. If there's one dominant horse in the race, play several exactas picking that horse in combination with three different horses in second place. If there's no clear standout, pick the three horses you think are best, then play all six possible exacta combinations.

6. Be consistent. "If you bet conservatively one race, then go with an exacta the next, you'll wind up pulling your hair out," says Beyer. "Pick a strategy and stick with it."

7. Don't play the long shot. "Consistently betting horses with 99-to-1 odds is the worst strategy possible," says Beyer.

8. Know your limit. When you go to the track, take only what you'd feel comfortable spending on a good dinner.

9. Hunt for a dark horse. "Once in a while oddsmakers overlook legitimate contenders," says Beyer. "If you see a horse that has a good speed figure *and* a good trainer, but he's at 15-to-1, don't be afraid to take a shot."

10. Look over the horses before the race. You can't predict a winner at first glance, but taking a walk around the paddock can help you make some tough calls. "A horse that has his head down and is sweating probably isn't a wise bet," says Beyer.

Poker

Russ Hamilton
Professional poker player and winner of the $1 million 1994
World Series of Poker

1. Know when to fold 'em. In draw poker, fold any hand that doesn't start with at least a pair of jacks, four cards of the same suit or four consecutive cards of a straight. In seven-card stud, fold if you don't start with at least a pair, three cards of the same suit or the middle three cards of a straight. Also fold a pair if an opponent raises on a pair that's higher than yours. "Good players play fewer hands and win more money," says Hamilton, who often cleans up playing only three or four hands a night.

2. When it's dealer's choice, choose seven-card stud. Being the last bettor in a round gives you an advantage because you can gauge the strength of your opponents' hands before placing your bet. And the more rounds, the bigger your edge.

3. Play the cheap tables. Professional poker players make their living preying on tourists at big-money tables, but they rarely bother with the lower-limit games. "When you're in a casino, stick to tables that have a maximum bet under $5," says Hamilton. "If you play no-limit or pot-limit games, you'll get destroyed."

4. Bet erratically. "Bad poker players bet the same way throughout an entire night," says Hamilton. Throw your opponents a curve by occasionally betting aggressively on a mediocre hand.

5. Watch for "tells." Little gestures can often give you a good indication of what kind of hand an opponent has. "To exude confidence, a bluffer tends to bet faster and splash his chips into the pot," says Hamilton. "Likewise, if a guy has a good hand, he'll deliberately stack his chips into the pot to make it look like he had to think about it."

6. Don't be neat. A good draw-poker player can identify what type of hand you have by the way you arrange your cards.

7. Memorize your hole cards. In stud poker, looking at your hole cards after every deal can give away valuable information. Say you're playing seven-card stud and you have a pair of tens in the hole and an eight of clubs up. You're dealt a king of clubs. Checking to see if one of your tens is a club tells your opponent you probably have a pair (because you weren't thinking flush and you should've folded if you didn't start with a pair), the pair isn't kings, and now you might be thinking flush.

8. Carry a big bankroll. If you're at a casino, you need to have about 100 times the upper limit of the table to survive the natural fluctuations in poker. So if you're at the $2 table, you'll need a $200 cash stash.

Football Pools

Norm Hitzges
ESPN football prognosticator

1. Avoid chronic losers. "Teams that are playing under .350 usually lose big and rarely cover the spread," says Hitzges. "Asking the point spread to save you in football is basically begging."

2. Don't take the underdog and 7.5. Half points are an oddsmaker's way of deceiving you into making a bad bet. "They want you to think you can take the underdog, lose by a touchdown and still win the bet," says Hitzges. "But the half point really says that the favorite is more than a touchdown better than its opponent." And in most cases, you'll do better taking the considerably stronger team and laying the 7.5.

3. Use reverse psychology. Consider taking the underdog and 6.5 points for the opposite reason. "In this case, the oddsmaker is telling you the favorite isn't a touchdown better than the underdog and the spread may easily make the difference," says Hitzges.

4. Avoid games with a 3.5 spread. "These games are usually too close to call," says Hitzges. But if you have to pick, lay the 3.5 and take the favorite for the same reasons given above.

5. Don't be fooled by the home-field advantage. Oddsmakers automatically give the home team three points. So if the home team is favored by only one or two points, it means the visiting team is actually the better team. "I'd take the stronger team over the home field any day," says Hitzges.

6. Bet on a good team after a bad game. A team's best performance and worst performance of the season often occur back-to-back. "If a usually successful team has an atrocious week that can't be attributed to injuries, you know they'll work really hard the next week," says Hitzges. What's more, oddsmakers will often give you a betting edge in these cases by giving a team that's just lost big an extra point or two in the next week's line. Conversely, be careful betting a team (especially one that's under .500) coming off a big win. They may be due for a letdown.

7. Look for big mismatches. When one team's greatest strength is pitted against another's biggest weakness, the game will usually be one-sided. "If the number one rushing offense is pitted against the 28th rushing defense, it's obvious who's going to control the game," says Hitzges.

8. Look for turnaround teams with good quarterbacks. Oddsmakers often underestimate losing teams on the comeback trail. "If a losing team is consistently competitive and has a quarterback who's posting good numbers, there's a good chance they'll turn things around," says Hitzges.

Blackjack

Arnold Snyder
Publisher and editor, *Blackjack Forum* magazine

1. Take a stand. If the dealer's showing a low card—a 2 through 6—stand on any hand 12 or higher. "With anything less than a pat hand (17 through 21) the dealer has to take an automatic hit," says Snyder. "And if he's showing a low card, chances are good he has a stiff hand (12 through 16) that can be busted with one card."

2. Hit if he's high. If the dealer is showing a high card—7 through ace—hit on anything less than 17.

3. Double down on 11. Doing so doubles your bet, but limits you to only one more card. "Because there are so many cards that can turn it into a 21, an 11 is one of the most valuable hands in blackjack," says Snyder.

4. Double down on 10 against 2 through 9. "A 10 is also a valuable hand in blackjack," says Snyder. "But if the dealer is showing a 10 or an ace, he has too strong a hand for you to double your bet against."

5. Always split a pair of aces or 8s. "Both are lousy hands and should be broken up into two separate hands," says Snyder. "You'll have to put bets on each, but starting with an 11 or an 8 is *far* better than starting with a 2, 12 or 16," says Snyder. One note: If you split a pair of aces, you'll get only one more card on each hand, and you can't double down. But on a split pair of 8s, you can take as many cards as you want on each hand. (And if you get a 3 for a total of 11, you can double down in some casinos.)

6. Never split a pair of 4s, 5s or 10s. "Only an idiot would break up a 10 or a 20, and starting with a 4 is worse than starting with an 8," says Snyder.

7. Don't always split the rest. "The sign of a true amateur is someone who splits all his pairs," says Snyder. For pairs of 2s, 3s, 6s, 7s and 9s, split only if dealer is showing a 2 through a 6.

8. Learn the basic strategy chart. Almost all blackjack books contain a chart that tells you what to do in every possible scenario. By learning the chart you can cut the house's

advantage to almost nothing. Consider this: The house's advantage over a novice runs between five and six percent; against an average player it's about two percent. Versus a guy who knows basic strategy, it's down to a mere half percent.

9. Don't chase your losses. The surest way to lose a bundle of money is to increase your bets to recoup your losses faster. "The house has the advantage, so pulling out more money doesn't guarantee you'll win your money back," says Snyder.

10. If you're playing at home, deal. "In home games, the dealer usually gets the ties," says Snyder. "That alone gives you an eight-percent advantage."

11. Don't play with strangers in private games. Unless you're at a reputable casino, avoid playing blackjack with guys you don't know. "It's nearly impossible to detect marked cards and good sleights of hand," says Snyder.

12. Count cards. Although most casinos—except the ones in New Jersey—can haul you out if they catch you, keeping a rough estimate of the cards that have been dealt, and betting accordingly, increases your odds of winning. "The more high cards left to be dealt, the more of an advantage you have and the more you should bet," says Snyder. "The more low cards there are in the deck, the more it helps the house and the less you should bet." Here's why: First, if you hit a natural 21—an ace plus a 10 or a face card—the house owes you money-and-a-half. If the house gets a natural, it doesn't win money-and-a-half. Second, the house has to hit hands 12 to 16, while you don't. So if there's more low cards left in the deck, the house has a better chance of making a hand.

13. But it ain't always that easy. The more decks the house uses at one time, the harder it is to get an advantage. "If the dealer is using six or eight decks, a rough counting system gives you less of an advantage than you think," says Snyder. "Unless you see several hands in a row full of low cards, it's probably not the best idea to start increasing your bets."

14. Skip the seminar. "Blackjack seminars that charge hundreds of dollars to teach you how to play the game are often hoaxes," says Snyder. The best way to improve your odds, he says, is to memorize the basic strategy chart available in any $15 blackjack book.

Chess

Joel Benjamin
Former editor, *Chess Chow* magazine. Grandmaster, U.S. Chess Champion (1987), currently ranked among the top 50 chessmasters in the world

1. Develop a few good openings. Because your first few moves set the tone for the entire game, it pays to learn a few well-designed openings from books or better players. "The key is to mobilize as many pieces as quickly as you can," says Benjamin. "Many novices only move a few and wind up suffocating themselves." As a rule, don't move the same piece twice in an opening—unless it's in danger or you can make a trade for a piece of equal or higher value.

2. Control the center. The four squares in the center of the board are the most important. From there you can fan out and control the entire board. "Start your siege in the center by occupying it with pawns," advises Benjamin. In general, the closer a square is to the center, the more meaningful it is.

3. Let your rook sit. Many beginners like to start the game by pushing their rook pawn to bring their rooks into play early. But that's the worst way to open, says Benjamin. It sets your rook up to be attacked early in the game, and you'll waste moves trying to evade your opponent. Instead, start with knights and bishops first—they're less valuable, so you can attack more freely.

4. Castle early. That tucks your king into a safe position and brings your rook to the middle of the board. "Nine times out of ten, you'll benefit by castling in the first 15 moves," says Benjamin.

5. Trade laws. When you're ahead, it's best to trade pieces of equal value. That's because the fewer pieces there are on the board, the less chance your opponent has of making a comeback. There's one exception, says Benjamin: "Don't trade pawns, because converting them to queens in the endgame can be the difference between a stalemate and checkmate." On the other hand, if you're behind, trade only for pieces of higher value and encourage exchanging pawns.

6. Corner his king. In the endgame, it's easiest to checkmate your opponent's king if you first force it into a corner. If that technique doesn't improve your endgame, consult a chess book—there you'll find standard methods for checkmating a king with various pieces.

7. Challenge yourself. "It's a waste of time to play someone you can beat all the time—no matter how much fun it is," says Benjamin. "The best opponents are players who are just a little better than you."

Crossword Puzzles

Will Shortz
Editor, *The New York Times* crossword puzzle

1. Start with the fill-in-the-blank clues and work out from there. Clues like "Man — — Mancha" (answer: of La) have the most definite answers, says Shortz. Plowing through all the clues in order increases the chance you'll make mistakes that will haunt you later.

2. Only guess in a pinch. A bad guess can lead to more mistakes, because once you fill in an answer you're less likely to doubt it. "Wait till you're stuck, then start guessing," says Shortz.

3. Use your eraser. "The biggest mistake people make is that they aren't willing to erase," says Shortz. "If you see circumspect letter combinations, like a 'j' next to a 'b', you probably need to change something or you're not going to get anywhere."

4. Resist the urge to fill in the s's and the ed's. While many plural and past tense clues end in s and ed, respectively, crossword-puzzle makers often look for unusual cases to throw you off. "Assuming a plural ends in s may help get you out of a hole, but it's not the best place to start," says Shortz.

5. Take a break. Putting the puzzle down and returning to it a couple of hours later can often break an impasse.

"Even if you think you're totally stuck, it's worth a try," says Shortz. "You may just get one more clue that will have you off and running again."

6. Know the archaic words cross-word-puzzle makers use. Because of their unusual combination of letters (particularly vowels), some words that are rarely used in real life pop up again and again in crossword puzzles. "I try my hardest to keep them out, but sometimes it's the only way to make a section work," says Shortz. Whenever you see an unusual three- or four-letter word, it pays to write it down for future reference. To get you started, here are some of the most common ones:

> Celebes ox: anoa
> Two-toed sloth: unau
> Soak flax: ret
> Sea eagle: ern or erne
> Arrow poison: inee
> Tokyo's former name: Edo

7. Look at the answers. If you're still stuck after taking a second look at your puzzle, check the answer key. "The fastest way to become a better puzzle-solver is to learn from your mistakes and omissions," says Shortz.

Darts

Larry Butler
World Match-Play Champion in steel-tipped darts, 1994

1. Watch the board, not the dart. "Your brain will automatically try to put the dart where you're focusing," says Butler. "If you're watching the dart leave your hand, you're focusing on the wrong thing."

2. Pace yourself. One of the biggest mistakes you can make in darts is to play at your opponent's pace. "Always concentrate on the target for one to two seconds before each throw," says Butler. "Other than that, find a comfortable rhythm and stick with it."

3. Get in the groove. If you pinch the dart between the pads of your index finger and thumb (as most peo-ple do), it can roll out of position as you throw it. Instead, place the dart between the pad of your thumb and the first groove of your index finger. For added accuracy, let the end of the barrel run against the first groove of your middle finger and rest the tip just underneath the fingernail of your ring finger. That way, your hand forms a cup around the dart. Having several cues will make it easier to hold the dart in the exact same position each time.

4. Stay back. You'll get more momentum if you hold the dart just behind its center than if you hold it dead center or slightly toward the front.

5. Learn proper technique. "Good dart players don't *throw* darts," says Butler. "They just give them a gentle push." Here's how to do it: With your upper arm parallel to the floor, cock your wrist back as far as possible so that the center of the dart is directly over your elbow. Then, keeping your upper arm still, bend your elbow to bring the dart back three or four inches (but not so far that it goes behind your eye). From there, let your forearm *fall* forward and give the dart a gentle push as its weight pulls it out of your hand.

6. Hold on loosely. If you have a tight grip, it's nearly impossible to release the dart at the same place every time. "Hold it as you would a baby bird," says Butler.

7. Trade in your glasses for contacts. Since the lenses of your glasses sit an inch off your face, they can create a minor distortion at eight feet. "It's not much, but every little bit counts in darts," says Butler.

8. Keep both eyes open. Closing one eye to aim the dart will throw off your depth perception and cause you to pull the dart off line.

9. Don't think of the consequences. When stepping to the line for a game-winning shot, it's natural to think about the implications of a bad—or good—shot. To keep your nerves from throwing you off, you have to improve your powers of concentration. Try this technique: Pick an object like a soda can and focus all your attention on that object for five minutes. (Set an egg timer or your watch alarm to keep you honest.) That will help you keep your mind from wandering during a match, says Butler.

LIVING

Getting a Good Shave

Christophe
Beverly Hills hairstylist who gave President Clinton his infamous $200 runway haircut

1. Get a straight-edge and a soap brick. They'll give you a smoother shave than any razor and foam. "We don't use them for nothing," says Christophe.

2. Shave after you shower, not before. A moist beard is much softer and easier to cut than a dry one.

3. Lather up. Working in your shaving cream with your hands or a soft brush maximizes the softness of your beard. "If you want a great shave, take 30 seconds to work it around in circles—don't just slap it on," says Christophe.

4. Go both ways. To get the closest shave, start by shaving in the direction your beard grows. Then go back and shave against the grain.

5. Listen to your razor. Most razors are good for only three or four shaves. "Once the blade starts tugging at your beard, it's time to change," says Christophe.

6. Double up. "Although you shouldn't always believe what you see on TV, double blades do shave closer than singles," says Christophe.

7. In a pinch, reach for the hair conditioner. If you run out of shaving cream, it's your best choice. Conditioner is thicker and lathers up better than soap and shampoo.

8. Skip the aftershave. "Aftershaves that contain alcohol don't do anything except burn and dry out your skin," says Christophe. Warm water is all you need unless you have unusually dry skin, in which case an aloe-containing moisturizer is in order.

9. Clean up your act. Granted, electric razors won't give you as close a shave as a blade, but if you're going to use one, remove the cutting heads at least once a month and soak them in alcohol. Otherwise, hair can get caught in the narrow spaces between the lifter and cutter and dull your shave even further.

Giving a Good Speech

Mario Cuomo
Former Governor of New York (1982–1994) and keynote speaker
at the 1988 Democratic National Convention

1. Don't read. "An audience wants you to talk to them and look at them," says Cuomo. If you read a speech, you're sure to be a bore.

2. Write it out. Putting a speech down on paper—and perhaps even rewriting it once or twice—will help you memorize what you want to say, so you don't have to read.

3. Bring the speech with you. "I always keep a full copy of the speech on the podium with the section headings in boldface," says Cuomo. "It's a good road map, but I often wind up adding anecdotes or elaborating on certain points if the audience looks bored or puzzled."

4. Have one clear message before you begin writing. "If you can't summarize the message of your speech in two sentences, you're not ready to begin writing—or speaking," says Cuomo.

5. Tell them why your subject is important. To get an audience's attention, start by clearly stating your message. Then immediately explain how it applies to them. "If I'm giving a speech about the budget to a nongovernmental audience, I'll say something like,

'This budget will save you money by cutting the taxes you pay. It will bring your schools more state aid to better educate your children. And it will help your local police fight crime to make your communities and your families safer,'" says Cuomo.

6. Keep it simple. "If you're talking to a roomful of people who aren't experts on the subject, steer clear of jargon and complex explanations," says Cuomo.

7. Paint pictures with your words. "To be successful, a speech has to provoke an emotional, as well as an intellectual, response," says Cuomo. "You can talk about AIDS simply by reciting a long list of grim statistics, or you could say, 'I've held AIDS babies—sweet, beautiful, bright-eyed youngsters—in my arms and fought back tears when I thought of the terrible shortness of their

lives.' By creating a word picture that puts a human face on a subject, you reach the audience in a way statistics alone cannot."

8. That's why Perot was so boring. Illustrating your points with words keeps your audience more engaged than displaying graphs or charts. Rely on visual aids only when you *must* talk about statistics, and then bring up only the most telling numbers.

9. Know your audience. If you're giving a speech to a group of people you don't know much about, ask the organizer to fill you in on a few of their major concerns *before* you write the speech.

10. Keep it as short as possible. If you're one of many speakers at a ceremonial event, 5 or 10 minutes is plenty. If you're the major speaker, 20 to 30 minutes is about right. Go longer only if it's absolutely necessary to fully cover your topic, or the organizer asks you to. "Someone once said 18 minutes is the ideal length for a speech—long enough to give them substance, but short enough not to bore them," says Cuomo.

11. Make your transitions smooth. If you introduce one point to help prove another, don't assume your audience will get the connection. It's your job to show them *clearly* how they're related.

12. Don't try to win an Oscar. "Voice inflection and gestures are necessary to bring your speech to life," says Cuomo. "But if you're overtheatrical, you'll come off as insincere."

13. Keep trying. Giving a good speech doesn't come naturally to anybody, says Cuomo. "Even the greatest speakers were once rank amateurs."

THE TEN BEST SPEECHES EVER GIVEN
Naomi Rhode
President, National Speakers Association

1. *Abraham Lincoln: Gettysburg Address.*

2. *John F. Kennedy: "Ask not what your country can do for you, but what you can do for your country."*

3. *Martin Luther King, Jr.: "I have a dream."*

4. *Jesus: The Sermon on the Mount.*

5. *Aristotle: "It was said, when others spoke they applauded, when he spoke the troops rose and went to war."*

6. *George Washington's farewell to the troops.*

7. *Winston Churchill: "Never, ever, give up."*

8. *Patrick Henry: "Give me liberty or give me death."*

9. *Margaret Thatcher: "A champion of world peace."*

10. *Paul Harvey: "Hello, Americans."*

Talking Your Way Out of a Speeding Ticket

David W. Kelley
Former California highway patrolman and author of *How to Talk Your Way Out of a Traffic Ticket* (CCC Publications, 1989)

1. Pull over as far as you can. The less risk an officer has of becoming road-kill, the more time he'll give you to explain your side of the story. "Never, ever, pull onto the median," says Kelley.

2. Know which excuses work. The best excuses are ones that paint you as a normally law-abiding driver who had a momentary lapse, says Kelley. If you ask him not to write you a ticket because "one more will put you over the edge," you'll set yourself up as a frequent violator and he's sure to nail you. The "racing-to-get-to-a-bathroom" and "running-out-of-gas" excuses rarely work, either.

3. Don't beg for mercy, and kill yourself before you cry. Neither of these behaviors are admirable to a guy who's spent his life dreaming of becoming a cop.

4. Be cooperative. Don't make a scene or say you're going to take your case to court—the less an officer remembers about the stop, the better chance you have of beating the ticket before a judge. "You may not always be able to talk your way out of a ticket," says Kelley, "but ignorance or a bad attitude will always talk you *into* one."

5. Sign the ticket. "Your signature is only a promise to appear in court to clear up the matter, not an admission of guilt," says Kelley. If you refuse to sign, the officer can arrest you and you'll blow any chance you had that he'd forget your case when it goes to court.

6. Take notes. If you do get a ticket, return to the scene a few minutes after the cop lets you go and jot down a few particulars about the road conditions. Were any road signs missing or obscured? Was there a center line? Was it solid or dotted? What were the road conditions? Was it sunny or cloudy? "If you're prepared, you have about a 50–50 chance of having the ticket thrown out or reduced, even if you're guilty," says Kelley.

7. Pictures help too. Photographs showing any obstructions or missing signs are often crucial in persuading a judge that you didn't deserve the ticket.

8. Ditch the radar detector. Even the most expensive radar detectors are no match for the instant-on radars and VASCAR systems police now use, says Kelley. But if you use one and get caught, always throw the detector under the seat. "If a cop spots a detector, it establishes you as a frequent violator who deserves the ticket," he says.

Holding Your Own in a Fight

Curtis Sliwa
Founder of the Guardian Angels

1. Run wisely. "Even if you have no intentions of fighting the knuckle-dragger in your face, don't take your eyes off him—or his buddies," says Sliwa. Instead of turning tail to run, move to the side or back away—then scram.

2. Keep the volume down. The biggest mistake you can make when someone is screaming in your face is to raise your voice in response. Not only will it fuel his fire, it'll cause you to lose control. "Stay calm and only hit him if you have to," says Sliwa.

3. Don't make a fist. "If you pop someone with a closed fist, you're likely to break your hand, giving your opponent a good chance to break your face," says Sliwa. Instead, use the palm of your hand or your elbow.

4. Go for the nose, not the nuts. Guys spend their whole lives learning how to protect the family jewels, but they're likely to leave their nose unguarded. "Even the slightest jolt to his schnoz will start his eyes watering and make him lightheaded," says Sliwa.

5. Cut your losses. If you get popped at the outset with a punch that wobbles your knees, make a run for it. "No matter how much you want to get even, once you get rocked with a good shot it's only going to get worse," says Sliwa.

6. Watch his shoulders. A twitch of the shoulders can tell you whether that big palooka is going to take a poke at you. "He can't kick you or punch you without moving his shoulders," says Sliwa. At the first sign of an attack, unleash an offensive of your own.

7. Strike first. If your gut (or his shoulders) tells you there's no other way out, it pays to take the first shot. "I'd rather have an appointment with a judge than a surgeon," says Sliwa.

8. Throw in a couple of wrestling moves. If a guy's getting the best of you and you can't get away, pull him close to your body and wrestle. The more time you spend rolling around on the floor, the more tired he'll get—and the more likely it is that someone will break it up.

9. Don't bluff. Don't pretend you're a tough guy if you're not. "The bigger you talk, the harder you're going to get clobbered when push comes to shove," says Sliwa.

10. Reach for protection. If a guy pulls a knife or picks up a bat, grab something to deflect his advances. Use anything—a chair, the top of a garbage can, even your jacket wrapped over your hands.

Training Your Dog

Bashkim Dibra
Dog trainer to the stars and author of *Dog Training by Bash* (Dutton, 1992) and *Teach Your Dog to Behave* (Dutton, 1993)

1. Use rewards, not punishments. The best way to get a dog to obey you is to reward him with praise or a treat when he listens, not to scream or hit him when he doesn't. If you catch him going to the bathroom on the carpet, say "no" in a firm voice and take him outside. Once he goes on the lawn, shower him with praise.

2. Never hit your dog. While it may get him to do what you want, it won't make him your best friend. "A scared dog isn't a happy dog," says Dibra.

3. Put him on a schedule. The easiest way to housebreak a puppy is to get him used to a routine. For the first two or three weeks, keep him in a large cage when you're not home. Make special trips home every three to four hours to put him outside for a bathroom break. Once he gets the hang of it, you can let him have the run of a whole room, but stick to your schedule—even on weekends. (If he has an accident inside the house, try the cage routine for another day or two.) If he goes two weeks without making a mess, he's ready for the whole house. But during the transition, be sure to keep him to his schedule. As he gets older and no longer needs to be confined in the cage, you can gradually prolong the time between his bathroom breaks until he can make it the whole workday.

4. Business before pleasure. When you take a puppy outside to go to the bathroom, don't play with him until after he does his duty. "At first, you want him to associate outside with bathroom, not play," says Dibra. Once he goes, praise him or give him a treat first—then you can play with him.

5. Don't send mixed signals. "To train a dog properly you have to be as disciplined as they are," says Dibra. "If you don't want him on the couch while you're at work, don't invite him up when you're there watching football."

6. Save the spoiling for later. The worst time to spoil a dog is when he's a puppy, says Dibra. "You want him to stick to

optimal behavior during programming," he says. "Then, when he's perfectly trained, you can spoil him a bit."

7. Tackle one thing at a time. Trying to teach a young dog too many behaviors at once will confuse him and make it difficult for him to learn anything.

8. Keep it to 15 minutes. Dogs have very short attention spans, so it's best to keep your lessons brief and repeat them several times throughout the day.

9. Use body language. It's easier for dogs to understand verbal commands when they're given in conjunction with hand or foot signals. For example, here's how to teach your dog the difference between "heel" and "stay": Each time you give the "heel" command, start walking away from your dog leading with your left foot. When you say "stay," walk away leading with your right foot. After a few lessons, your dog will associate your foot movements with the proper command.

10. Put his toys away. To let your dog know which toys are his and which are yours, always keep his together in a box where he can get at them easily. And if you want to protect your new Nikes, don't give him an old shoe to play with. "Puppies have a hard time telling the difference between an old shoe and a new one," says Dibra.

11. Get a dog that fits your lifestyle. "It's almost impossible to mesh with a dog if you're different creatures at heart," says Dibra. If you're extremely active, border collies, labs, shepherds, retrievers and hounds are good choices. If you get off the couch only to go to the fridge, you'll do better with a basset hound, bulldog or St. Bernard.

Buying a Suit

Giorgio Armani
Italian suitmaker and designer

1. If you're going to buy only one suit, make it blue. Every man should have a dark blue or navy soft wool suit with a flattering cut. "It looks great with a T-shirt or a print shirt, but it can also serve for important occasions when worn with a white shirt and a tie," says Armani.

2. Pick a lightweight backup. "A second suit should be in a neutral color like beige, taupe or dove grey—colors that look good on everyone and with everything—in a light fabric like viscose or a tropical-weight wool," says Armani.

3. Your suit shouldn't make a statement. "Avoid buying any suit tied too closely to seasonal trends," says Armani, "including jackets made in strange shapes or unusual fabrics, and patterns that are too loud or contain overly bright colors."

4. Use accessories to express your originality. "Wear a scarf instead of a tie. Add a vest. Try a collarless shirt or one with a Nehru collar. Or swap your shoes for a pair of boots or moccasins," he suggests.

5. Buy off the rack. If you don't have a "drop" (the difference in size between your shoulders and your waist) of over eight inches, or unusually wide shoulders, you can almost always buy a good suit off the rack and save the cost of a tailor, says Armani. Try on a few suits to see how you look in different cuts—and when you're making your decision, pay more attention to the mirror than the salesman.

6. Show some sleeve, but no socks. Your jacket sleeve should expose a half inch to an inch of your shirt sleeve. Your pants are the proper length if the hem rests on the tops of your shoes so that there is just a gentle break or crease at the ankle.

7. It's better to buy big. If you do have to go to a tailor, it's better to buy a bigger suit and have it taken in than to snatch up a smaller one that needs to be let out. "A suit isn't an accordion that can be expanded without visible consequences," says Armani.

8. Don't be a stuffed suit. Cramming yourself into a smaller suit to hide a couple of pounds (or to make yourself feel better about wearing a smaller size) has just the opposite effect—it draws more attention to your girth. Instead, pick a suit that's a little fuller in the shoulders and tapers slightly to your waist. "You may not be able to hide those extra pounds totally, but you can make sure your suit doesn't announce them," says Armani.

9. Double-breasted jackets aren't for everyone. "As a rule they don't look good on short men and guys who have a spare tire," says Armani.

Getting Your Kid into College

David L. Evans
Senior admissions officer at Harvard University

1. Put grades first. Great SAT scores can't make up for mediocre grades. "A 1,500 SAT score with a C+ average shows a lack of discipline," says Evans. "And Harvard is not a place for an undisciplined person."

2. Don't flood the admissions office. Avoid sending more than three extra recommendations (beyond what is required). "In general, the heavier the application, the lighter the applicant," says Evans. "We don't need to know all the details of your life, just the highlights."

3. Forget the résumé. Send one only if it covers something you couldn't fit into your application, and keep it to one page.

4. Tie it up. The most important thing in applying to college is to show how everything in your application ties together. "Meld your personal qualities, academic achievements and extracurricular activities into one appealing package," says Evans.

5. Don't do everything. While colleges pay a great deal of attention to extracurriculars, it doesn't mean you have to be a part of every club your high school has to offer. "It's much better to spend a lot of time on one true passion than to spend half an hour a week in fifteen different activities," says Evans. "We look for leadership."

6. Send samples. If you've started a business or won awards for writing poetry, music or producing a video, send a *brief* sample of your work along with your application. "A while ago we graduated a woman who ran her own bakery and sent us a loaf of bread with her application," says Evans.

7. Know your recommenders. "While we seldom see negative letters of recommendation for students, we're not impressed with form-letter types that contain little personal information," says Evans. During your junior year in high school, make it a point to sit down and talk with the people you plan to ask for recommendations. That will help them get to know you better. Or, write them a letter explaining why you want their recommendation and mention activities and accomplishments about which they may not know.

8. Do the best with what you've got. While all universities evaluate the strength of an applicant's high-school curriculum, they're more concerned about how well the student did in the classes that were offered. "We look to see if the student took the more rigorous courses at his school," says Evans. "But we don't recommend switching schools to try to get into college. If your curriculum is very weak, you may want to take some courses at a local college or attend a summer program."

Brewing Beer

Jim Koch
Master brewer and owner of Samuel Adams Boston Lager,
named the Best Beer in America at the Great American Beer
Festival, 1991–94

1. Clean up your act. "The first rule of home brewing is sanitation," says Koch. Sterilize your equipment with Clorox and hot water before each brewing, or you'll never make good beer, he says.

2. Buy the best hops. Good hops are the most important ingredients in beer, says Koch. Noble hops like Hollertau Mittlefruh, Bohemian Saaz and Tettnang Tettnang are the best for lager. They'll prove to be worth the extra money come taste time. If you're making ale, go with Kentish Goldings or Kentish Fuggles. Even good hops can spoil if they are exposed to heat or light, so make sure the ones you buy are cold-stored in vacuum-sealed foil pouches.

3. Malt is important too. Using a quality malt will help you produce a quality beer. "Two-row malt will produce a smoother, better-tasting beer than six-row malt," says Koch. If you can't find a good home-brewing supply store in your area, two high-quality mail-order suppliers of hops and malt are: James Page Brewery in Minneapolis (800) 347-4042 and Home Sweet Homebrew in Philadelphia (215) 569-9469.

4. Start simple. Darker, more flavorful beers like stout, steam beer and dark ales are the easiest to make because small mistakes are often concealed by the strong flavor. Lagers, on the other hand, have more subtle flavors that give you no room to hide.

5. Be cool during fermentation. Fermentation temperature will peak 24 to 72 hours after the process begins. During this time it's critical to keep the room temperature below 60 degrees Fahrenheit. "If your basement isn't that cool, get an air conditioner," says Koch. "You can't make good beer in a warm basement."

6. Learn from your mistakes. If your beer ends up with a buttery taste, it got too warm during fermentation. A sour or vinegarlike flavor tells you there's bacteria in your brew and you need to sterilize your equipment more thoroughly.

7. Don't eyeball the sugar. After the beer is finished fermenting, make sure you add the *exact* amount of sugar called for in your recipe. Sugar restarts the fermentation process and gives beer its carbonation. "A bit of sugar can be the difference between creating great beer and making grenades," says Koch. "If you don't add enough, the beer will be flat, but if you add too much, the bottle will blow up."

RELATIONSHIPS

Making Conversation

Larry King
Host of "Larry King Live" and author of *How to Talk to Anyone, Anytime, Anywhere: The Secrets of Good Conversation* (Crown, 1994)

1. Always appear interested. "The surest way to endear yourself to a person is to look into their eyes and appear to be genuinely interested in what she has to say—even if she's talking about the shrimp sauce," says King.

2. Play dumb. A good strategy to strike up a conversation with a total stranger is to play a little naive on a popular topic in the news and ask him to fill you in. "For example, when the O. J. Simpson trial was going on, you could say you were busy or out of town and didn't catch the latest facts," says King. "That always works. People love to be the expert."

3. Ask about her job. It's the next best thing to bringing up a juicy story that's in the news. "I've never met anyone who didn't like to talk about her work," says King.

4. Give a nod. People love to be affirmed when they're talking, so giving her a nod every once in a while can make both of you feel more comfortable.

5. Be a good listener. "The biggest mistake people make in conversation is to talk too much about themselves," says King. "What you do is usually most interesting to you. Don't use the word 'I' until you're asked."

6. Avoid yes-or-no questions. Questions that can be answered with one or two words fail to draw out reluctant talkers. Instead, ask questions that begin with "why."

7. Know what's taboo. In general, people don't like negative conversation. "At cocktail parties, never put down the host," says King. "And whenever you talk to the boss, don't complain about other employees. If you want to bring up a problem, ask him what he would do in your shoes."

8. Ditching a jabberjaw. If someone's got your ear in a vise-grip, you can always resort to surefire escape tactics like looking past her shoulder and saying you see somebody you need to talk to. Or glance at your watch and use the old I've-got-to-make-a-phone-call excuse, King advises.

9. Go slow. "It's OK to pause before you answer someone's question," says King. "You're not in court, where the answers are expected to be on the tip of your tongue. Think about what you want to say."

Picking Up a Woman in a Bar

Jenny McCarthy
1994 *Playboy* Playmate of the Year

1. Be patient. "The surest way to get shot down is to come up to a girl right away and say, 'You're so beautiful, can I buy you a drink?'" says McCarthy. Instead, stay about 20 feet away, try to make eye contact and give her a smile. If she does a double take or returns the smile, it's a green light to approach. If she turns around and never looks back, move on.

2. Make eye contact, don't stare. "Staring makes people nervous," says McCarthy. Gaze her way every few minutes until she sees you. Hold the look for about three seconds, then turn away.

3. Don't be overcomplimentary. Telling her she's the most beautiful woman you've ever seen sounds insincere, even if it isn't. It's best just to introduce yourself and offer to buy her a drink. Later in your conversation you can say something nice about her smile or her hair.

4. Don't assume she's thirsty. Walking up to a woman and asking "What are you drinking?" comes off as pretentious. If you want to buy her a drink, ask whether she wants one first.

5. Be a good listener. When you first meet a woman, don't try to give her all the details of your life. "Women love guys who listen to them," says McCarthy. If you hear your voice more than hers, start asking her questions.

6. Play your cards right. If you have only a few seconds to make your pitch and give her your phone number—say, in a cab or on the street—handing her your business card with a little note on the back is OK. But in a bar, where you have more time to be social, it can kill your chances. "I'd rather a guy try to impress me with his personality than his credentials," says McCarthy.

7. Take a friend, not a pack. When you're out to meet a woman, it's best to bring along one or two of your buddies. "If you're with six guys, it looks like you're in a contest, and if you go in alone, the woman thinks, 'If his friends won't go out with him, why should I?'" says McCarthy.

8. Respect girl talk. Never, I repeat, *never*, approach a girl when she's in deep conversation with her girlfriends. "Even if you were Alec Baldwin, I'd shoot you down if you interrupted some heavy gossip," says McCarthy.

9. Look, but don't touch. Women are often intimidated by physical contact. The more gentlemanly you are, the better your chances.

10. Dress down. Wearing clothes that make you stand out is dating death. "I like to see a guy in solid colors, like a black shirt and jeans with maybe a blazer," McCarthy says. "Lots of stripes or bright colors will make you look like you're Larry from 'Three's Company.'"

11. Avoid exotic dancing. Kill yourself before trying to impress a woman you don't know with your John Travolta moves on the dance floor. "I'd rather be with a guy who's a little awkward than somebody who's all over the place," says McCarthy. "As long as you can move your hips and feet to the beat, you'll be all right."

12. Don't hound. "If you get shot down once, it's over—move on," says McCarthy. If you keep bugging a woman, other women will notice and you won't get *any* action.

Best Pick-up Lines for Different Situations
Sharyn Wolf
Author of *Guerrilla Dating Tactics: Strategies, Tips and Secrets for Finding Romance* (Penguin Books, 1993)

ON THE STREET

The ground rules: Address her safety concerns and put the next move in her hands.

Pickup tactic #1: Ask her how to get to a place in the same direction she's going. Chances are, she'll tell you to walk with her, giving you time to introduce yourself and tell her your true intentions. In a real pinch, you can hand her a business card (to give her more information about you) and ask her to call you if she'd like to go out for dessert or coffee. Before you give her the card, flip it over and jot down your home phone number so that she knows you're not married.

Pickup tactic #2: Take the direct approach. Say, "I don't want to scare you, but I was afraid I would never get to see you again." Then ask her to call you and hand her your card. On the back, along with your home phone number, add a note that says, "This card good for one free ice cream cone—nontransferable." "A little creativity goes a long way," says Wolf.

AT WORK

The ground rules: Use your connections and be very, very careful.

Pickup tactic #1: To pick up someone you don't work with closely, find out what some of her interests are. Then stop.by her office and ask her about it: "Hey, I heard you like to water ski. So do I. Where's your favorite spot?"

Pickup tactic #2: When you're interested in someone you work closely with, you can be walking a fine line between romance and harassment. With a coworker of equal or higher status, the truth is your best option. Say something like, "I know this is awkward, but I'd like to spend some time with you outside of work. Would that be uncomfortable for you?" Asking an employee you supervise out on a date can be career suicide. Don't do it unless you're confident you want her to be your wife.

AT A PARTY

The ground rules: Parties are the easiest place to pick up a woman because everyone feels they're connected to the host in some way. Use it to your advantage.

Pickup tactic #1: With strangers, look for the common bond, using questions like, "Are you a friend of so-and-so?" or "How do you know so-and-so?"

Pickup tactic #2: If you know the woman casually, tell her about a new movie you just saw or a new restaurant you discovered and ask her what she's done lately that she's really enjoyed. Or play naive about a popular current events topic and ask her to fill you in.

IN A BAR

The ground rules: People go to a bar because they don't want to be alone. Being entertaining can work to your advantage.

Pickup tactic #1: Stupid-but-witty lines can often buy you a smile and some conversation time. A classic: "So, do you think we'll ever convert to the metric system?"

Pickup tactic #2: If you've already made eye contact and she seems at least somewhat interested, the standards "May I buy you a drink?" or "Would you like to dance?" are suitable strategies.

Making Dinner for a Woman

Graham Kerr
Host of "The Graham Kerr Show" and author of several
cookbooks, including his latest, *Graham Kerr's Kitchen*
(Doubleday, 1994)

1. Lighten up. "The heavier the meal, the deeper the sleep," says Kerr who still woos his wife of 50 years with two special dinners every month. Serving a low-fat meal will keep her from wanting to call it a night as soon as she polishes off dessert.

2. Don't be too fancy. As with speeches, simpler is better. A well-prepared piece of fish or chicken with a simple vegetable on the side is much more appealing than a piece of meat swimming in a thick sauce, says Kerr.

3. Bake your own bread. Not just for its flavor—the strong, pleasant aroma of a fresh loaf will make her feel comfortable and cozy as soon as she walks through the door. (The easy way out: Invest in a bread machine.)

4. Have food on the table. A simple appetizer waiting for her when she arrives will make your table look much more attractive, says Kerr. "I like to lead off with a plate of smoked salmon served with thinly sliced pieces of toast, cut diagonally with crusts trimmed, and very lightly buttered," he says. "I'll throw a lemon quarter on the plate with a small fork already in it, and maybe even a Hawaiian orchid for extra color."

5. Cover your tracks. Although it's nice to offer a woman a glass of wine at the start of the meal, it can make her think you have ulterior motives. To prove to her that you're a stand-up guy, give her the option of a nonalcoholic wine. "Ariel Vineyards in Napa Valley has an exquisite selection," says Kerr. If she's not the wine type, juice, mineral water, or sparkling water are good alternatives.

6. Question her. Just because you consider your Super Bowl chili the house specialty doesn't mean she's going to like it. To make a dinner really special, you have to "draw a road map to her taste buds," says Kerr. Find out her food preferences so that you can create a meal just for her. What are her favorite seasonings?—garlic? cilantro? oregano? Favorite fruits and vegetables? Does she like meat, fish or poultry, or is she a vegetarian? Is she partial to Thai? Mexican? French? How does she like her foods prepared—baked, broiled or stir-fried? Any cookbook worth its salt should be able to help you come up with a recipe based on the information you've obtained, says Kerr.

7. Perfect your presentation. How your table looks says as much about your feelings for her as the food. Start with two tablecloths, one round and one square. The bottom one should be larger and fit the shape of your table, the top one smaller to provide some contrast. "I like plain tablecloths in soft colors like white on tan, or beige on chocolate," says Kerr. Match your napkins with the bottom tablecloth, and serve your food on plain, white plates so it stands out as much as possible.

8. Douse the candles. "While they're a splendidly romantic idea, candles cast thoroughly unflattering shadows on both you and your food," says Kerr. A dim light placed directly over the middle of the table is best.

9. Ditch the roses and gardenias, too. Having fresh flowers on the table is a must, but these strong-smelling types can cut into the taste of the food. Instead, go for flowers with little or no scent—like Hawaiian orchids or large daisies. "Eating is as much an olfactory experience as a taste experience," says Kerr.

10. Keep it to three courses. An appetizer (preferably cold), an entrée and dessert are all obligatory. If you have to have a salad, serve it after the entrée. "It's very European, and assures peaceful digestion," says Kerr.

11. Never practice. By risking failure, you prove to her exactly how much she means to you, says Kerr.

Making Love to a Woman

Anne Hooper

Sex therapist, former editor of *Penthouse Forum* and author of *The Ultimate Sex Book* (Dorling Kindersley, 1992) and *Anne Hooper's Kama Sutra* (Dorling Kindersley, 1994)

1. Ask for input. If she hesitates to tell you what she wants, or says, "Anything's OK," you can assume she probably has a hard time expressing her desires. In that case, try different things and ask if what you're doing feels good. "The more detailed a map you can draw of her body, the better lover you'll be," says Hooper.

2. Tell her what you like. If a woman feels like she's giving you pleasure, she'll be more willing to let you please her. "If you like to be touched in a certain way, tell her directly or give her some sign of appreciation when she does," says Hooper.

3. Know how to redirect her. If she's doing something you don't particularly enjoy, it's not always a good idea to tell her to stop. Instead say, "That would feel much better over here," and gently move her hand.

4. Rub her the right way. Giving her a 15- to 20-minute massage before intercourse can help her get warmed up sexually and improve the experience for both of you. Start with a fairly firm touch and slowly lighten up until you're just running your fingernails across her entire body. "If you do it right, it's very, very erotic," says Hooper.

5. Break from tradition. We tend to stick with certain patterns of lovemaking we know usually work well for us, says Hooper. Unfortunately, relying on the same old methods can kill your desire *and* hers. But a complete overhaul isn't necessary. A subtle change, like stroking her with your left hand instead of your right, can make a big difference.

6. Make a date. Kids, work and stress could kill even Casanova's libido. Getting a baby-sitter and spending half the night in a fancy hotel can do wonders for livening things up.

7. Get wet. The first time you make love to a particular woman should be as unhurried as possible, says Hooper. Taking a warm bath or shower together beforehand is a good prelude. "If you're not ready for that, you're probably not ready to sleep together either," says Hooper.

Raising Good Kids

Ron Taffel, Ph.D.
Director, family and couples treatment, Institute for Contemporary Psychotherapy, and author of *Parenting by Heart: How to Stay in Charge and Connected with Your Kids* (Addison-Wesley, 1991)

1. Be there for the little things. "You can't really bond with your kid if you just show up for the all-star game or final dance recital," says Taffel. To really show your kid you care, take on some of the more traditional "mommy" tasks, like bandaging cuts and bruises and picking up your kid from school if he's sick. Or take a few hours out of your day to watch a soccer practice.

2. Make discipline logical. All successful discipline methods have a common thread—logical consequences. "If your kid's acting up at the dinner table, it doesn't make sense to say, 'No movies for a month'—that's just not enforceable and the punishment doesn't fit the crime," says Taffel. Instead, say something like: "If you keep acting up, you won't get to watch your favorite show tonight," or send him to his room for an hour—not the whole evening. "That way, he'll take you more seriously," says Taffel.

3. Admit your mistakes. Kids, especially young ones, think the world revolves around them. So if you go home in a bad mood and explode at him for something little, he'll blame himself and his self-esteem will suffer. Once you cool off, go back and explain to him that you were in a bad mood and it wasn't his fault. "Good kids have parents who are responsible for their actions," says Taffel.

4. Don't spank. The problem with spanking is that it works *too* well, says Taffel. "It makes the kid afraid of you, so he's less likely to approach you with his problems." Also, kids can develop a tolerance to spanking—the more you use it, the less they respond and the more likely they are to say, "Go ahead, hit me." Only spank your kids when they put themselves in danger, such as when they run out into the street, or if they're hurting another child, says Taffel.

5. Resist the urge to pounce. When your kid finally gets up the nerve to approach you about a sensitive issue, don't drop everything and say, "Let's talk." Most likely, he'll feel too much pressure and clam up. Instead, acknowledge his presence, but stay somewhat involved with what you're doing. "Unless they're really upset, kids will talk best when you're not staring into their eyes," says Taffel.

6. Give advice. Kids want to know how you really feel, so *tell* them—don't just parrot what they say and ask them how they feel. Show preteens you understand their situation by telling similar stories about yourself. Take the opposite tack with teenagers. "Teens are in the business of differentiating themselves from their parents," says Taffel. So instead of saying "I know exactly how you feel," start off with "It was totally different when I was a kid, but here's what I might do."

7. Limit TV to one-and-a-half to two hours a day. "Scientific studies show there's a direct relationship between the amount of TV kids watch and how they do in school," says Taffel. Kids who watch a lot of TV may also be more likely to be depressed and bored. If they tend to watch educational programming—not junk—you can allow them an extra half hour.

8. Have your kid tested. If he's doing well in some subjects, but poorly in others, it's usually not a sign of laziness or poor study habits. He may have a slight problem with his visual memory, for example, that can be easily corrected. If you suspect a problem, have your kid tested as early as possible—preferably in the second or third grade. "Kids who don't understand why they can't grasp certain things can wind up with major self-esteem problems later in life," says Taffel.

9. Don't overcompensate for the sins of your parents. "If you weren't allowed to speak up as a kid, it's not a license to give your kid free rein," says Taffel. On the other hand, don't try to be exactly like your parents. "Probably the biggest mistake in parenting is allowing yourself to be overshadowed by the past and not seeing your kids for who they are."

Making Up (Without Losing Your Pride)

John Gray, Ph.D.
Psychologist and author of the best-seller *Men Are from Mars, Women Are from Venus* (HarperCollins, 1992) and *What Your Mother Couldn't Tell You & Your Father Didn't Know* (HarperCollins, 1994)

1. Don't say, "I'm sorry" or tell her she's right. Quick apologies are often seen as insincere shortcuts for ending a fight—so doing it too soon is usually counterproductive. "Women want to feel like they're being listened to," says Gray. "The best thing you can do is to listen to her side of the story until she cools off; then apologize if you want."

2. Hold off on the excuses and explanations. Again, women need time to be upset. "If you try to explain why you're not a jerk before she's had a chance to present her entire argument, you're more likely to convince her that you are one," says Gray.

3. Touch her. "Placing a gentle hand on a woman's shoulder and initiating conversation takes away 50 percent of the emotional charge," says Gray. If she's not upset with you, she'll melt in your arms. If she is, she'll pull away. At that point, don't get upset or try to touch her again—just ask her to talk to you about it.

4. Don't try to solve her problems. Even if she's not upset with you, offering a woman quick-fix solutions will make her feel that you're minimizing her feelings. "Hear her out and then help her find an answer," says Gray.

5. Forget counterattacks. If she starts bombarding you with critical comments, do your best not to attack back. "If you don't react negatively, she's more likely to think her accusations are wrong," says Gray. If she keeps it up, tell her you want to hear what she's saying, but ask her sincerely if there is anything that you're doing right.

6. Be a calm negotiator. "Yelling, screaming and throwing things are the worst communication skills possible," says Gray. If you can't control your temper, tell her you need a few minutes to cool off. Take a walk, and then resume negotiating.

7. Get her on your side. If you still disagree with her after she airs out her grievances, start your rebuttal by recapping her arguments with a question like, "Am I right to say that you're upset because . . ." Doing so gets her to agree with you on something and makes her feel that you've listened and are trying to work with her, says Gray.

Acknowledgments

To my family, Salomon, Barbara and Natalie for their support and confidence. And to Lisa Delaney, for all her editorial wizardry and patience. I love all of you.

Special thanks to my agent Arielle Eckstut of James Levine Communications and Jim Levine, Melissa Rowland, and Daniel Greenberg without whose urgings and hard work this project would never have been conceived. Also, to my editor, Brian Tart, for his tireless efforts on my behalf. And finally, much gratitude to my illustrator, Mark Matcho—a man who appreciates late-night revisions as much as I do.

About the Author

DAN BENSIMHON has been at the forefront of health-and-fitness writing for the past five years, during which he served as the associate editor of *Men's Health*. He's also completed nearly 100 marathons and triathlons, including the Hawaiian Ironman. Currently, he's a contributing editor/writer for *Men's Journal* and attending the University of Pittsburgh Medical School.